Best Poems of 1962

BEST POEMS
of 1962

BORESTONE MOUNTAIN POETRY AWARDS
1963

*A Compilation of Original Poetry
published in
Magazines of the English-speaking World
in 1962*

FIFTEENTH ANNUAL ISSUE

VOLUME XV

*Barry College Library
Miami, Florida*

PACIFIC BOOKS, PUBLISHERS • PALO ALTO, CALIFORNIA

1963

Pacific Books, Publishers
Palo Alto, California

© 1963 by Borestone Mountain Poetry Awards
All rights reserved
Printed in the United States of America
Library of Congress Catalog Card Number: 49-49262

ANNOUNCEMENT OF AWARDS AND ACKNOWLEDGMENTS

This is the fifteenth volume of Borestone Mountain Poetry Awards' annual selections and awards. The reading staff recommended nearly three hundred poems out of several thousand originally published in approximately two hundred magazines throughout the English-speaking world. Translations and poems of over one hundred lines are not con-considered. According to our usual procedure, the recommended poems were submitted to the judges with the names of the poets and publications deleted, since no pattern of selections is desired or intended.

The first award of $300 goes to Jean Burden for her poem "Poem Before Departure." John Haag receives the second award of $200 for his poem "Jonah." "An Unborn Child" by Derek Mahon receives the third award of $100. As in the past, poems that are among the final selections but not entered for the awards are so noted in the Table of Contents.

The editors wish to express their appreciation for the splendid co-operation of the magazines that publish poetry, and we gratefully acknowledge permission to reprint these selected poems from the magazines, publishers, and authors owning the copyrights. Poems requiring special forms of citation are listed below.

The Editors

Lionel Stevenson, *Chairman*
Howard Sergeant
  British Commonwealth Magazines
  (except Canada)
Waddell Austin, *Managing Editor*

Hildegarde Flanner
Gertrude Claytor
Frances Minturn Howard

Gemma d'Auria

"Poem Before Departure" by Jean Burden is reprinted from *The American Scholar*, Volume 32, Number 1 (Winter 1962–63), copyright © 1962 by The United Chapters of Phi Beta Kappa; use of the poem is by permission of the publishers. The poems "The Fortress" (page 132), "Sandpiper" (page 19), "The Dusk of Horses" (page 47), "By Canoe through the Fir Forest" (page 45), "Pigeon Woman" (page 140), "Division" (page 123), and "Rhinoceros" (page 135) © 1962 The New Yorker Magazine, Inc. "A Letter" by James Dickey is from *The Sewanee Review*, Volume LXX, Number 3 (Summer, 1962).

"God Germed in Raw Granite" by Brother Antoninus, originally selected from *The Commonweal*, appears in his collection of poems *The Hazards of Holiness*, copyright © 1962 by Brother Antoninus and reprinted by permission of the author and Doubleday & Company, Inc. The poem "Saetas de Dolores" by Suzanne Gross was selected from *The Commonweal* and later included in her book, *Sands Verbena*, published by The University of Notre Dame Press, September, 1962. "The Moslems' Angel of Death" by Thomas Merton also appears in his book, *Emblems of a Season of Fury*, copyright 1962 by The Abbey of Gethsemani, Inc., and is reprinted by permission of New Directions, Publishers. "The Far Field" by Theodore Roethke, originally published in *The Sewanee Review*, Volume LXX, Number 4 (Autumn, 1962), was also published in the December 21, 1962 issue of *The Times Literary Supplement* (London). "The Fortress" by Anne Sexton, originally selected from *The New Yorker*, is also from her recent book, *All My Pretty Ones*, and is reprinted by permission of Houghton Mifflin Company as well as the author.

CONTENTS

		PAGE
Jean Burden (First Prize): POEM BEFORE DEPARTURE *The American Scholar*—Winter		3
John Haag (Second Prize): JONAH *The Hudson Review*—Winter		4
Derek Mahon (Third Prize): AN UNBORN CHILD *Icarus* (Ireland)—December		7
Dannie Abse: ODD *The Poetry Review* (England)—Spring		9
Milton Acorn: I SHOUT LOVE *The Canadian Forum* (Canada)—May		11
Evelyn Adams: NIGHT CALLER *The Fiddlehead* (Canada)—Winter		16
Brother Antoninus: GOD GERMED IN RAW GRANITE *The Commonweal*—June 15		17
Elizabeth Bishop: SANDPIPER *The New Yorker*—July 21		19
Sam Bradley: LAST HOUR OF THE SENTRY REPTILES *The Kenyon Review*—Summer		20
Sam Bradley: SUPERSTRATA *Friends Journal*—January 1		21
David Bromige: ALICE IS THE LOOKING-GLASS *The Canadian Forum* (Canada)—December		22
George Mackay Brown: THE SAILOR, THE OLD WOMAN, AND THE GIRL *The Paris Review*—Summer-Fall		24
Maurice Carpenter: A COUNTERBLAST TO YEATS' "SECOND COMING" *Outposts* (England)—Spring		25

		PAGE
Charles Causley:	A SHORT LIFE OF NEVILL NORTHEY BURNARD *New Statesman* (England)—November	27
Gordon Challis:	THE ANONYMOUS MAN WRITES A LOVE-LETTER *Landfall* (New Zealand)—September	30
Robert Chrisman:	SWAN LAKE *Contact*—June	32
Robert Conquest:	ON THE MIDDLE THAMES *Poetry Northwest*—Spring	35
Louis Coxe:	BREAKING THE BARRIER *Poetry*—November	38
James Dickey:	A LETTER *The Sewanee Review*—Summer	41
James Dickey:	ARMOR *The Hudson Review*—Winter	43
James Dickey:	BY CANOE THROUGH THE FIR FOREST *The New Yorker*—June 16	45
James Dickey:	THE DUSK OF HORSES *The New Yorker*—December 1	47
William Dickey:	AT BEDTIME *The Kenyon Review*—Summer	49
William Dickey:	NOT THIS *Northwest Review*—Fall	51
Maurice Duggan:	CALYPSO *Landfall* (New Zealand)—March	52
Charles Edward Eaton:	SOME, NOT ALL *Northwest Review*—Summer	55
Michel Farano:	DIRGE FOR HILDA DOOLITTLE *The Lyric*—Winter	56

		PAGE
Robert Francis:	DOLPHIN *The Massachusetts Review*—Spring (Mr. Francis' poem not entered in Contest)	58
Robert Francis:	THOREAU IN ITALY *The Massachusetts Review*—Spring (Mr. Francis' poem not entered in Contest)	60
Raymond Garlick:	NOTE ON THE ILIAD *The Anglo-Welsh Review* (England)—March	62
Brewster Ghiselin:	BLACK VULTURES OVER GUAYMAS *The Kenyon Review*—Winter (Mr. Ghiselin's poem not entered in Contest)	64
Zulfikar Ghose:	THE BODY'S INDEPENDENCE *The London Magazine* (England)—April	66
Suzanne Gross:	SAETAS DE DOLORES *The Commonweal*—December 21	68
Donald Hall:	IN THE KITCHEN OF THE OLD HOUSE *Poetry*—April	70
John Heath-Stubbs:	A POET IN NEED *The Poetry Review* (England)—Autumn	72
Charles Higham:	THE WAR MUSEUM AT NAGASAKI *Quadrant* (Australia)—No. 4	74
John Holmes:	EDWARD HICKS'S OLD PICTURE *Harper's Magazine*—February	75
John Holmes:	FAITHFUL READER *Harper's Magazine*—July	77
A. D. Hope:	THE YOUNG GIRL AT THE BALL *Meanjin Quarterly* (Australia)—No. 2	78
Graham Hough:	NEWS FROM THE CITY *The Critical Quarterly* (England)—Winter	80

		PAGE
Daniel Hughes:	THOSE TWO	82
	Quarterly Review of Literature—Vol. 12, No. 1-2	
Ted Hughes:	SUGAR-LOAF	84
	The Atlantic Monthly—May	
Kay Johnson:	FROM: THE FOURTH HOUR	85
	The Outsider—No. 2	
Carolyn Kizer:	BY THE RIVERSIDE	87
	Prairie Schooner—Winter	
Carolyn Kizer:	LOVEMUSIC	89
	Prairie Schooner—Winter	
Maxine W. Kumin:	SISYPHUS	90
	The Hudson Review—Spring	
Konstantinos Lardas:	WITH OPEN LOVE	92
	Prairie Schooner—Winter	
Richmond Lattimore:	CLAUDIA GOODBYE	94
	The Virginia Quarterly Review—Autumn	
Oswald LeWinter:	OH THE COSSACKS	96
	Contact—June	
Michael Longley:	DAY OF DANCING	98
	Icarus (Ireland)—March	
George MacBeth:	REPORT TO THE DIRECTOR	101
	The London Magazine (England)—January	
Mark McCloskey:	LOVE POEMS	103
	Wormwood Review—No. 6	
William Meredith:	FABLES ABOUT ERROR	105
	The Hudson Review—Spring	
Thomas Merton:	THE MOSLEMS' ANGEL OF DEATH	108
	The Commonweal—June 1	

		PAGE
Josephine Miles:	PROMOTER *Uclan Review*—Spring	110
M. Morris:	SITTING SERIES *The Canadian Forum* (Canada)—March	113
Philip Murray:	INNOCENTS *The Commonweal*—May 25	117
Leonard E. Nathan:	FOR MY SON, TEN *Epoch*—Winter	118
Sylvia Plath:	FACE LIFT *Poetry*—March	119
Sylvia Plath:	PRIVATE GROUND *Harper's Magazine*—August	120
Sylvia Plath:	WUTHERING HEIGHTS *New Statesman* (England)—March 16	121
John Ratti:	DIVISION *The New Yorker*—February 17	123
Theodore Roethke:	THE FAR FIELD *The Sewanee Review*—Fall	124
Eric C. Rolls:	THE HARE *Poetry Magazine* (Australia)—December	128
Alan Ross:	NELSON AT PALERMO *New Statesman* (England)—December	130
Anne Sexton:	THE FORTRESS *The New Yorker*—September 22	132
William Stafford:	LAKE CHELAN *The Hudson Review*—Spring	134
Adrien Stoutenburg:	RHINOCEROS *The New Yorker*—April 21	135

		PAGE
Nancy Sullivan:	Weighing the Heart of the Scribe Ani *Southwest Review*—Spring	136
Hollis Summers:	Seven Occasions for Song *The Hudson Review*—Spring	138
May Swenson:	Pigeon Woman *The New Yorker*—October 13	140
Lilian Symons:	The Albino Man *The Canadian Forum* (Canada)—July	142
Lilian Symons:	The Well *The Canadian Forum* (Canada)—October	143
A. S. J. Tessimond:	Heaven *The London Magazine* (England)—August	145
Sister M. Therese:	A Light of Revelation to the Gentiles *The Commonweal*—December 28	147
D. M. Thomas:	The Day before the Last *Unicorn* (England)—Spring	148
Constance Urdang:	Lines for My Grandmother's Grave *Quarterly Review of Literature*—Vol. 12, No. 1-2	149
Vernon Watkins:	Triads *Poetry*—October-November	151
Francis Webb:	Harry *Meanjin Quarterly* (Australia)—No. 1	153
Marie de L. Welch:	Salamander *The Beloit Poetry Journal*—Winter	155
David Wevill:	The Space Flier *The Listener* (England)—March 8	157
Harold Witt:	After the Snake *The Kenyon Review*—Spring	159
Exta Williams Wolking:	Metamorphosis *Approach*—Summer	160

Best Poems of 1962

POEM BEFORE DEPARTURE

This place moves from me
like a slow tide pulling out
against the moon.
It does not matter if I push up earth
against the door,
or turn the key within the lock;
even as I lean,
the tree trembles in the wood,
the pebble flies within the rock.

Or if I stay like a crouched animal
within,
I watch the walls move back,
grow membrane-thin;
leaves sprayed against the pane
blur a little at the edge;
vines pale and loosen on the sill.

It does not matter that I prop beneath the knob
tables, chairs.
Something recedes
that once was still;
what was mobile, stares.

The time is soon,
though I, longing to be caught by root
or weed,
resist departure as a kind of death.
Something began and ended here.
One morning, whether I dare or do not dare,
I shall look up, unroofed, to sky;
I shall gaze through timber
that once I leaned my fear against—
and knock on air.

Jean Burden

JONAH

*The waters compassed me about, even to the soul:
the depth closed me round about, the weeds were
wrapped about my head.*
—Jonah II, 5

*

Below the level of the reasonable eye
What presses most—the darkness or the sea?

That light that left me when I left the light
No longer bears me up; sodden, my weight

Sinks to the sea floor. I am leather-lunged;
I squeeze a stopped heart with a spasmodic hand.

These garlands of sargassum clutch my skull;
Thigh-deep, the grey-green streamers flow and swell,

Glowing in a sinuous meadow, slow
As gestation . . . I should remember where they go—

These tendrils, tendrils, tendrils—as they turn
And sway in the current. I am water-worn

And the hair on my hands lives like anemones
Or the beards of crabs; a jelly films my eyes;

Even my bones grow soft as bladderwrack.
A thallus anchors rootless upon the rock;

I slip from rock, glide to the rim—the depth.
Black violets blooming in the serpent's mouth,

Tongues of decay, a pulpy garden—all
Pass into shadow, darkening as I fall.

When did I choose to do this torpid dance
Of a brine-breather? Good air, I knew you once,

But now my spongy tissue will not rise.
Father, the sky is more than I can loose.

     * *

Who has found the limits of liquid? or the end
Of weeds? Warm-blooded breathers of the wind,

I tell you there's no bottom to the sea.
The feather and the stone bruise equally

In this fluid hub the darkness turns upon.
A nerve worms through the entire flesh to spawn

In the belly; a touch sets the gall afire
And kindles the unknown heart . . . Out of that lair

The final monster comes: blind as the waters,
From a swollen mouth and roots of hair it gathers;

Out of the self, unseen, unseeing, flows
That secret beast that swallows as it grows.

And I, engulfed in entrails, stiffen, bend,
Am limp again, am eel, slug, jelly—unboned,

Quiescent, listening to the tick of salt
Till, pressed by the pulse that beats in all things wet

I wait, quickening with the lust for lungs.
Is it time to move? The monstrous tallow clings

But my weedy shroud revives an older heat;
And, when I stretch, constraining tissues knot

Then quiver, expelling me like ambergris
On white and sun-hot sand. In a light place

I lie, new as a leaf, while bones unbend,
The flesh grows firm, and my hair dries in the wind.

JOHN HAAG

AN UNBORN CHILD
(for Wendy)

I have already come to the verge of
Departure—a month or so and
I will be vacating this familiar room.
Its fabric fits me almost like a glove
While leaving latitude for a free hand.
I begin to put on the manners of the world,
Sensing the splitting light above
My head, where in the silence I lie curled.

Certain mysteries are relayed to me
Through the dark network of my mother's body
While she sits sewing the white shrouds
Of my apotheosis. I know the twisted
Kitten that lies there sunning himself
Under the bare bulb, the clouds
Of goldfish mooning around upon the shelf.
In me these data are already vested—

I feel them in my bones, and they embrace
Nothing, for I am completely egocentric.
Such pandemonium of encumbrances
As will absorb me, mind and senses—
Intricacies of the box and the rat-race—
I imagine only. Though they linger and,
Like fingers, stretch until the knuckles crack,
They cannot dwarf the dimensions of my hand.

So whether I am to take the shape of a beast
Or a beauty—whether my habitual style
Be choler, phlegm or yellow bile—
Bounty, or secrecy of poltergeist

And the black teeth of the galactophile
Lacing its blood with rot—although
I toy with ways and means—I do not know.
These things are all in the future. Meanwhile

I must compose myself in the nerve-centre
Of this metropolis, and not fidget—
Although sometimes at night, when the city
Has gone to sleep, I keep in touch with it
Listening to the warm red water
Running in the sewers of my mother's body—
Or the moths, soft as eyelids, or the rain
Wiping its wet wings on the window-pane.

And sometimes too, in the small hours of the morning
When the dead filament has ceased to ring—
After the goldfish are dissolved in darkness
And the kitten has gathered itself up into a ball
Between the groceries and the sewing,
I slip the trappings of my harness
To range these hollows in discreet rehearsal
And, battering at the concavity of my caul,

Produce in my mouth the words I WANT TO LIVE—
This my first protest, and shall be my last.
As I am innocent, everything I do
Or say is couched in the affirmative.
I want to see, hear, touch and taste
These things with which I am to be encumbered.
Perhaps I need not worry—give
Or take a day or two, my days are numbered.

DEREK MAHON

ODD

In front of our house at Golders Green
the lawn, like a cliche, mutters 'Rose bushes.'
The whole suburb is very respectable.
Ugly men drive past in funeral suits,
from their necks you can tell they're overweight.

Sodium lamp-posts, at night, hose empty roads
with gold which treacles over pavement trees,
polishes brittle hedges, clings on closed, parked cars.
If a light should fly on in an upstairs room
odds on two someones are going to sleep

It's unusual to meet a beggar,
you hardly ever see a someone drunk.
It's a nice, clean, quiet, religious place.
For my part, now and then, I want to scream;
thus, by the neighbours, am considered odd.

From the sensible wastes of Golders Green
I journey to Soho where a job owns me.
Soho is not a respectable place.
Underweight women in the gamiest of skirts
bleed a smile of false teeth at ugly men.

Later, the dark is shabby with paste electric
of peeporamas, brothels, clubs and pubs,
restaurants that sport sallow waiters who cough.
If a light should fly on in an upstairs room
odds on two someones are going to bed.

It's customary to see many beggars,
common to meet people roaring and drunk.
It's a nice, loud, dirty, irreligious place.
For my part, now and then, I want to scream;
thus, by Soho friends, am considered odd.

DANNIE ABSE

I SHOUT LOVE

I shout Love in a land muttering slack damnation
as I would in a blizzard's blow,
staggering stung by snowfire in the numbing tongues
 of cold,
for my heart's a furry sharp-toothed thing
that charges out whimpering
even when pain cries the sign written on it.

I shout Love even tho it might deafen you,
and never say that Love's a mild thing
for it's hard, a violation
of all laws for the shrinking of people.
I *shout* Love, counting on the hope
that you'll sing and not shatter in Love's vibration.

I shout Love . . . Love . . . It's a net
scooping us weltering, fighting for joy,
hearts beating out new tempos against each other.

The wild centre life explodes from a seed
recreates me daily in your eyes' innocence
as a small ancient creature, Love's inventor,
listened to a rainbow of whispers.

I shout Love against the proverbs of the damned
which they pause between clubbings and treacheries
to quote with wise communicative nods . . . I know
they're lies, but know too
that if I declared a truce in this war
they'd turn into pronged truths and disembowel me.

I shout Love against my prison where unconscious joy
like a brown sparrow chirping hoppity zig-zag
seems my keeper . . . In his bright ignorant eye
I live a prisoner while masons plonk stone
to soak up sunlight meant for prisoners
each one a piece of my brain, fragment of my heart's
    muscle:

And prisoners with hunger aching like a tooth in the
    belly;
        All the robbed ones—
wonderless kids,
    strengthless men,
        women with no vision for their womb-thoughts.
How'll I escape? Clang shut my own cell door?

I shout Love even in this city
where you don't dare breathe thru your mouth.

Even I shout Love who aged ten thousand years
before my tenth birthday,
in shame, wrath and wickedness;
shout and grow young as cowards grow old:
shout Love whom the world's paradoxical joy
makes stammer or keep silent between shoutings,
more held each hour by the wonder of it.

I shout You my Love in a springtime instant
when I wince half pain half joy to notes from an oriole
over balls of frost trapped in quickening roots,
and the tick-tock-tickle of warm rain
trickling into buds' eyes, plucking them open.

I shout Love into your pain when times change and you
    must change:
minutes seeming final as a judge's sentence
when skies crack and fall
like splinters of mirrors
and gauntle'd fingers, blued as a great rake
pluck the balled yarn of your brain.

The herring with his sperm makes milk of the wide
    wrinkling wriggling ocean
where snowy whales jump rolling among whitecaps
as I shout live your Love and the deeds of my words
pollinate the air you're breathing.
Since life's a dream garment hung singing or sighing
    on a bone tree
why shouldn't it be Love's adventure?

I shout Love between your knees that are my wings
    of Love,
when I ride like a dragon
blessing you fierce as curses.
Oh take me Love for I'm a storm of light
enwhorled with satanic darkness.

I whisper Love into the ear of a newborn girl,
breathing Love in her name.
May she grow up around her name singing inside her.

I shout Love against Death, that rattling, stinking
    harvest machine
that loves best the gentlest and ripest in Love.
I've seen their eyes bright with hunger
gorgeing on their last light;
and felt Love lurch sidling away
from the small help they wanted.

I shout Love and am no sentimentalist.
for I rejoice in the deaths of rogues.

But Love life thrilling roots
like nerves digging the buried corpse,
the old fierce eye rotted and born new,
an enemy lost in a lover.

I shout Love wherever there's loveless silence;
in dumb rocks, in black iron lie oppressed minds
like parsecs of night between the stars,
where suns in tumultuous sleep toss eruptions about
    them
and I wake with a cry
spinning among the galaxies.

I shout Love to the young whose eyes are clouded with
    light
as their light clouds my eyes.
Only as beards of wheat swaying at the fingertips may
    I touch them
for they're born in the centre, are the centre,
and I shout Love, even tho
there's something of me they must destroy.

I shout Love at those grey-lipped men who trim life:
Shout Love into their dim tears, their shaking heads.

I shout Love to you, flesh humming thoughts, blood's
    rhythm,
intricate bonework, hair played in by wind,
and your words jostling, seeking
things growing or still, people'd mysteries, yourself
with your soles touching the grass for instants.

I Love the dawn, with a half-risen sun all rosy like the
    head of God's phallus.

But what if I came shouting Love now
to you shivering in your blanket
unfed for forty-eight hours?
The liberals goggle over their cocktails
to talk patiently of feeding you,
but I shout Love and I mean business.

I shout Love in those four-letter words
contrived to smudge and put it in a harmless place,
for Love today's a curse and defiance.
Listen you money-plated bastards
puffing to blow back the rolling Earth with your
    propaganda bellows
            and oh-so-reasoned negations of Creation:
When I shout Love I mean your destruction.

                                MILTON ACORN

NIGHT CALLER

A field mouse stopped by the door last night,
After the storm; I see his track
Of four light feet and a line between
Where his tail dragged snow as he stole unseen
Across the pasture from woods out back.

His trail meanders from side to side
As if he were staggering from a blow;
It might have been moonlight through a pine
That struck on his eyes as it struck on mine
When I woke to the stillness that follows snow.

If he clawed at the door, I didn't hear;
He's one of a crowd who scratch about
After walls and warmth—but I just assume
What he wanted—perhaps inside the room
He sensed a creature that dreamed of out.

Evelyn Adams

GOD GERMED IN RAW GRANITE

God germed in raw granite, source-glimpsed in stone?
Or imaged out in the black-flamed
Onyx-open line? Smouldered in the tortured
Free-flow of lava? The igneous
Instant of conception? As maiden-form
Swells in the heaviness of wold, sleeps
Rumped and wanton-bulged in the boulder's
Bulk, is shaped in tree-forms everywhere
As any may see: dropped logs, say, or those crotched
Trunks, pronged like a reckless nymph
Head-plunged into the earth—so Godhood
Wakes under water, shape-lurked, or grave and somber,
Where sea falls, mocks through flung foam. . . .

                                                  Ghost!

Can this be? Breather of elemental truths
She stirs and coaxes! Out of my heart's howk,
Out of my soul's wild wrath
I make oath! In my emptiness
These arms gall for her, bride's mouth,
Spent-breathed in laughter, or that night's
First unblushing revealment, the flexed
Probity of the flesh, the hymen-hilted troth,
We closed, we clung on it, the stroked
And clangorous rapture!
                              I am dazed.
Is this she? Woman within!
Can this be? Do we, His images, float
Time-spun on the vaster drag
His timelessness evokes?
In the blind heart's core, when we,
Well-wedded merge, by Him
Twained into one and solved there,

Are these three? Are three
So oned, in the full-forthing
(Heart's reft, the spirit's great
Unreckonable grope, and God's
Devouring splendor in the stroke) are we—
This all, this utterness, this terrible
Total truth—indubitably He?

BROTHER ANTONINUS

SANDPIPER

The roaring alongside he takes for granted,
and that every so often the world is bound to shake.
He runs, he runs to the south, finical, awkward,
in a state of controlled panic, a student of Blake.

The beach hisses like fat. On his left, a sheet
of interrupting water comes and goes
and glazes over his dark and brittle feet.
He runs, he runs straight through it, watching his toes.

—Watching, rather, the spaces of sand between them,
where (no detail too small) the Atlantic drains
rapidly backwards and downwards. As he runs,
he stares at the dragging grains.

The world is a mist. The world is uniquely
minute and vast and clear. The tide
is higher or lower. He couldn't tell you which.
His beak is focussed; he is preoccupied,

looking for something, something, something.
Poor bird, he is obsessed!
The millions of grains are black, white, tan, and gray,
mixed with quartz grains, rose and amethyst.

Elizabeth Bishop

LAST HOUR OF THE SENTRY REPTILES

Being unbrokenly busy, I did not notice
the drizzle falling on the small
monsters. The uncomfortable floor was all
earth. I had just uncovered my latest
immemorial plan and had set it, constellated,
amid the death masks. Its greatest
rubies were Mars-red.
                            Even the servants were
vibrant with discovery; as if answering drums,
their words soared and trumpeted. "Up
comes the treasure," they shouted; "up comes
the sacred vessel." I recoiled, aghast
at ecstasy held in such common clay.

We worked easily, once past
historic layers—and feverishly. I did see
the softly padding little monsters sway
in the foreign phlogiston air. Tasks
done, their phthisis come, they flickered red tongues
quite void of terror, and did not try to flee
to gray bowels of humility,
once stronghold, now our possession.

Being pre-diluvian, they were soon dust; we
were too excited to think to save one
specimen for a natural history
museum. And no one made intercession
for creatures obviously meant
for oblivion.

SAM BRADLEY

SUPERSTRATA

"How can we take
ground of our lost year?"
                      The lichen
                      does not penetrate
                      the stone.

"Can we force our time
to make our meaning clear?"
                      Beneath sea-roar,
                      a tolling undertone.

"I sleep no more:
I dream morosely here."
                      Nerves fret
                      against firmness
                      of flesh and bone.

"After raid, after panic,
soon the shrill:
  All clear!"
                      Reality,
                      a weak state
                      overthrown.

"Crisis crowds us."
                      Wind
                      is fetid with fear.

"Will our sons follow us?"
                      Are they freeborn?

"Will they remember us
tomorow morn?"
                      History trembles,
                      futile as a tear.

"Will names of turntide—"
                      (inscribed on
                      bronze and brass?)

"—tell of our brotherhood?"
                      (beneath the grass?)

                          Sam Bradley

ALICE IS THE LOOKING-GLASS

The sleek head emerges
from a coney coat
so fortunately short
that I can gaze
on her melon knees
as she sits down,
till
    her eyes cross mine
as the taut face turns
through ninety degrees:

that blue beam betrays
no recognition,
not of me as a man
 (well okay then)
but not as an organ-
                    ism, either:

The Distant Look,

which she next fixes on
her stocking-seam—
and Look! there's the same
remoteness in her touch.
She holds her leg
like a stranger's hand
or a brand-new crutch,
or it grew on someone else.

I've been depicting
its continuity
             and here she

is handling its lines
as if it didn't arch
beneath all barricados
of metal and elastic
to sheathe in her loins
in avocado softness—

   does it swing on steel hinges?
   I'm sure she's saying to it,
"Don't know where YOU sprang from,
   still I'm glad you match
   the rest of my
              accessories.
   Now don't you let me down!"

And at night I can see her
in the dim pink room
unpinning each long limb,
unscrewing from her head
the honey-golden beehive,
aligning every part
on the soft thick quilt,
like a row of dolls,

   turning all the lights up,
   staring distantly
            until
   those eyes begin to focus
   on all the ordered charms:

then she
       folds up the face,
peels off the hands

sinks into her own zinc arms.

                              DAVID BROMIGE

THE SAILOR, THE OLD WOMAN, AND THE GIRL

"Have you any cure," cried the young sailor
  Pulling against the tide,
"Have you any herb or spell to help
  This new pain in my side?"

The old woman gathering whelks
  Raised her fierce gray head,
"The best cure in the world for that
  Is, take her to your bed.

"If that won't do, there's two fine places
  To end a lover's moans—
The ale-house with its lamp and barrel,
  The kirk-yard with its stones.

"Or use the black worm of the mind.
  Think, when she leans up close
And all the lurings of Delilah
  Break open like a rose

"Against your lips and throat and eyes,
  That I am lying there,
Time's first lover stark as a thorn,
  In a white winter air."

The girl sang from another shore
  And the sweet oars beat on,
And the old woman laughed and struck
  Like roots through the gray stone.

GEORGE MACKAY BROWN

A COUNTERBLAST TO YEATS' "SECOND COMING"

"The best lack all conviction and the worst
Are full of passionate intensity."

Pouring my passionate intensity
Into the crucible where all convictions
Are molten in the mould of poetry,
I grope for gold in the slag heap of each
Victory's fiction, discovering myself
One of the worst who burn and cannot rest
Till dreams transmuted by this chemistry
Work in the world, uncovering her wealth
In wastes, and warming spaces with her aching zests.

My Adam by the Alchemist evicted
Shoulders the gold of his intensity,
Matter grows passionate from contradiction
Whose touch blows up a blaze of poetry
And Lucifer involved in chemistry
Is crucified, and all his hoarded wealth
Locked in a coffin. Adam's hand is pressed
Into the beaten ground of towns, himself
Created; enclose a green zest that is Eden's echo.

By dreams disordered thought is poetry.
Man, rampant anarchist, continually evicted
From his dreaming skull, quarrels with history
And lifts the pillars of his glittering fiction
Above the nexus of a blind inaction.
Back in the skull the wash of all his zest
Gathers, bright bubble, round the grain where friction
Grows a covering pearl, the grist of chemistry
Guilded and built, becomes a reviving mystery.

One of the worst, who grope for their conviction
In a waste of words, a wanderer in the nexus
Of galaxies, seeking for passionate
Matter within the common atom's echo
I know the good I thought was chemical
Is changed to a strange glow on strange faces,
And this whole complex, once mechanical
Becomes an image washed in mystery,
Pushed by the hand of history out of the mist.

MAURICE CARPENTER

A SHORT LIFE OF NEVILL NORTHEY BURNARD

CORNISH SCULPTOR 1818–1878

Here lived Burnard who with his finger's bone
Broke syllables of light from the moorstone,
Spat on the genesis of dust and clay,
Rubbed with huge hands the blinded eyes of day,
And through the seasons of the talking sun
Walked, calm as God, the fields of Altarnun.

Here, where St Nonna with a holy reed
Hit the bare granite, made the waters bleed,
Madmen swam to their wits in her thin well,
Young Burnard fasted, watched, learned how to tell
Stone beads under the stream, and at its knock
Quietly lifted out his prize of rock.

As Michelangelo by stone possessed
Sucked the green marble from his mother's breast
So Burnard, at his shoulder the earth's weight,
Received, on his child's tongue, wafers of slate
And when he heard his granite hour strike
Murdered Christ's hangman with a mason's spike.

The village lay still as a marriage bed,
Gulls from the north coast stumbled overhead
As Burnard, lying in the church-yard hay,
Summer-faced, corn-haired, hacked childhood away,
On the tomb slabs watched bugler, saint, dove,
Under his beating fists grow big with love.

The mortar-boy with the Laöcoon's snake crown
Caught with a six-inch nail the stinking town.
He turned, as Midas, men to stone, then gold.
Forgot, he said, what it was to be cold.
Birds rang like coins. He spread his fingers wide.
Wider the gulfs of love. His child died.

Packing only his heart, a half-hewn stone,
He left house, clothes, goods, blundered off alone:
London to Cornwall and the spinning moor,
Slept in stacks, hedges, barns, retraced the spoor
Of lost innocence through the shallows walking,
Of his dead child, they say, for ever talking.

At last, the dragged November sun on high,
Burnard lay down in a mumpers' inn to die,
At Redruth Workhouse with the stripped, the insane,
Banged on death's door and did not bang in vain,
Rocked in a paupers' gig to a sleep of clay
Where three more warmed his side till judgement day.

No mourner stood to tuck him in God's bed,
Only the coffin-pusher. Overhead,
The fishing rooks unravelling the hour,
Two men, a boy, restored Camborne Church tower.
'This box,' said the clerk, 'holds one of your craft
   in place'.
'We come,' they said, 'to smooth the dirt from his face.'

No cross marks the spot where Burnard first saw day.
Time with a knife wears stone and slow flesh away,
Peels the soft skin of the blocks he cut on the green
Signing himself, 'Burnard. Sculptor. Aged thirteen.'
Snakes still hiss in the Laöcoon. The sea's gun
Sounds over Cornwall. His eyes stare down from the sun.

The torn tramp, rough with talents, enters the park.
Children have stones at the ready. Men and dogs bark.
The light falls into the bay, the cold sea leaks,
The slate face flushes, opens its lips, speaks.
In from the moor the terrible shadows flock,
Finger, beneath the stream, the innocent rock.

                                        CHARLES CAUSLEY

THE ANONYMOUS MAN WRITES A LOVE-LETTER

I have forgotten how to write my name
and therefore, if this letter
falls in hands
of some blackmailing scoundrel such as time
who threatens: 'You had better
pay or else'—or else he will proclaim
its contents to the public, I shall stand

some distance in the shadows, only known
as Mister X, the cryptic
Mister X—
of such pervasive fame and virile line,
his mention sends electric
whispers round the gallery whose own
desires will be defined and fit the text.

It's said that time will tell; indeed he may;
meanwhile I'll scan the slender
arc of chance
that still my signature might come to me
and you then know the sender.
If we meet, I do not know what way
I can invent to catch your unplanned glance.

My voice is like the noise in libraries
of lonely men who fritter,
book by book,
the aimless pages, which they scarcely see,
more random than the scatter-
gram of rain; who, driven, dread to freeze
inactive, or to choose, if someone looks.

My face is like a composite of shots
of preselected features,
some my own,
assembled then in sections, stuck on sheets
and put away for future
reference but lost among a lot
of other faces, captionless, unknown.

My life and death give no hint of their game,
show no trace of correlation,
show, in fact,
a sort of independence which would seem
to fit my spark's ablation,
best charted by an X—my present name
in absence of the one I lost, or lacked.

I feel if I could meet you, see you whole
and you could see me likewise,
time, for shame,
would turn a blinded eye. If I could trail
the summer through its gateways
to where you rearrange the sunlight's role,
I would remember how to write my name.

Gordon Challis

SWAN LAKE
To Gale

I

The world of difference wounds the eye
Like a beak, a chatter of tongues
Assails the ear and mouth
Of dumb desire, that cannot speak
The honied syllables of hunger,
Dying like a fish in excess of water.
Love falls back upon itself,
A salmon sinking with its ebb
Into a well of undistorted water.

And thinking of this now in sunshine
And blue skies, and of the purple iris
In my garden whose sudden bloom surprised me
Like a piece of sky on fire;
How she shocked again this morning when
My eye sought hers in her bed of earth
And found her crisp and curled as paper ash;
I wondered on the substance of her love,
That did not seek my garden nor deny it,
And graced it until death disgraced her flesh;
Thinking of this now and of that bulb,
My heart, I want to learn about dirt.

II

She rises in the waters of my memory
Like a swan who lingered in my river,
Sang her song and fled one morning
On the white bell-beating of her wings.
And thinking of those wings and sheets,
Our bodies murmuring so drowsily
They seemed to be the wind in summer leaves,

She fades before me like a dream I dreamed
For days and nights incessantly
Of white sea waves and fading blue.

And now the angel exorcised in the eye of dawn,
Who was no woman but a vaporous Helen,
Seed of swan and silver shuck of god,
I turn and see the sunshine wash the lawn
And hear again my footsteps in our room
Of chittering birds and empty streets
When the dark bed held us like an acre of earth
And in the womb we blossomed white.

I think of Ulysses and the olive tree
That held his bed, and did he hear the branches
Rustling overhead like Sibyl's leaves?
The white bones in our body will destroy us,
For every year I feel the bone
Come nearer to the front I show the world.

III

When what we love are white birds
And white horses winging, singing into sun
Until the heart is a mane of wind,
And when that swan sings her final note,
When the unicorn is lacquered into carousels,
When all this glory is enamel and ash,
What shall we find in a human face?

Your eyes revive in me those irises
That bloom forever, not watered by wine
Nor fed on feathers, but children to the sun.
You shimmer with your light like burning marble,
Hard hips hooked like horns around your rose,
Your breasts the bread of children
And the blossom of my years.

You carry an egg within you,
Round, white and full as the sun,
And being bone and flesh,
How can its plumage wither?
A river of swans and horses shall be yours
And fly from your limbs like breath.
The day darkens and like pieces
Of a shattered egg, I see a flood of white wings
Circle in the sky and hear the winter geese
Beating like bells as they return.

Robert Chrisman

ON THE MIDDLE THAMES

To translate life, the working of pure chance
Induct consummate harmony for once:
With all components clear,
    Shine, flow, think, feel
    Assembled to a chord.
    First, air: those hours' ambience,
Bright on steep woods, the reach of stream, the weir,
    Raised to a higher power
    —Astonishing, unseasonable
Weather that has to sing
Chanced adagios of
Luck that a time of love
Should meet, should be, the exceptional
Days of a Berkshire spring.

Everything becomes landscape, becomes love.
Love flows . . . But watch the ponded drifts above
The weir that change as they slip
    Through sluice, down overflow.
    Not formless: annealed
    By the play of several forces
Ephemeral substance pours through steady shape.
    Squeezed to metal, shattered to spray,
    Chopped to breaking, thrown to surging,
Waters explicitly sing,
Not in bare metaphor
But belled beneath the weir
Where those whitely converging
Currents sweep and swing.

Bright differentiations! Though they go
Spun back to gleaming unities of flow,

Always light meshes tense
    Stressing the frame of things
    As it too fragmentates
    In cruxes of devolution;
Blues from high dust, blurs bright from leaves and skins,
    Fans rigour of the single radiance
    Till all the air's one transfinite:
For light may be said to sing,
Even in its most discrete
Reduction the photon strikes
Through what all grand mathematics
Pure to the senses bring.

And transitory. Another night is blest,
And it is morning. Pull the curtains. West
Swans float on flux and form enough
    Beyond our window. But here
    More sensuous than all waters,
    More abundant than all radiance,
Everything, even landscape, becomes love.
    I need only burn in your breath
    To hear the great tune woken:
Love is a way to sing
Various yet unbroken
A cool flow, no less flame,
That bell-like fire, its chime
With which the world-weirs ring.

But can we find essential metaphor?
We may go down to Marlow, in an hour
See the same water soar
    Another arc . . . Though analysis
    Be a high sweetness too,
    Why must such correspondences
Sound clearer yet what life is structured for?

    Streaming symbol, sparkling cypher
    Stress more the pure original?
—Life finds its way to sing
Beyond all self, all sense:
This mere experience,
This chime of the most real.
Thank you. Thank everything.

                                  ROBERT CONQUEST

BREAKING THE BARRIER

THE BASE COMMANDER CONTEMPLATES TIME AND SPACE

Angels ten thousand! Men scramble on the ground,
The AA puffs like winter breath and we sail
A metal cloud far above pursuit,
Eye on the bombsight, hand on the toggle switch,
The bays to the cave of the winds opening on cold
And the quaint city foreign and far below. . . .
We jump with bomb-release after our run—
Twelve o'clock high and diving—never again,
No more fighters, no more Zeros dancing
The leap of their boresighted deadly guns.
Lie still, Nippon. Close your eyes girl and pretend
Our weight is love—
           —All right, all right.
Am I better off awake?
           A man's dreams
Must sag of their own weight as they grow older:
Night soil.
           I can walk this dead ground floor
And look out over the dark field like a prairie
Watching the big ones down from SAC patrol
And the others hand over silver hand into dark
All of them armed. As we were armed that day—
No one dreaming then what shaken spores
From the blown fungus would foul the world we breathe.
The barrier breaks; fifty thousand angels
Leap on the pinpoint of those vapor trails—
Presque Isle, Goose Bay, Reykjavik, the North Cape
And down the latitudes.
           Release should lighten and leap.
V-J Day. . . . Where was my way out?
I stayed in, my heart shorted like a solenoid,
I stayed trapped in the bay, not free to fall.

Go back? I had held the old world in my hand.
There was no outside, only dead center: I stayed—
Some since then, bailing out of guilt,
Fell swinging on their madness like a 'chute
But never found their ground. The new world's inside,
At the center of fire a cold bay that can fling
Incredible centigrades in spores, vapor and dust. . . .
I can see it falling, even as we leaped and banked
Sixty degrees in a tight turn, counting it down.
God rested that day on us, his second thoughts.

I hear planes on the apron, Navy Banshees,
Waiting for first light and their seaward leap
Back to the carrier. All hands alert,
The LSO and the mirror lift them down
Like heirlooms—not for themselves but what they mean.
—I should go back to bed. No more dreams,
Not till another night.

                Was I like them—
The cropped hair, tile-blue eyes and warrior's mettle?
We are all the same, class after class, hard, mindless,
Mirrors of myself homing me down
To the hardstand where the men of power and will
Choose me again for their whirl and plasma worlds.

Now I command here, fifteen years of light
Away from Tinian, Iwo, the last run.
                        Angels thirty thousand
Dance in sunlight over Hiróshima . . .
Cold in the bomb-bay. Who was the one who knew
Of all on board what monster foal we'd drop . . . ?
Bigger now, and the planes. All of us obsolete.
I dropped the warrior's headstone. Slogans we wrote
On the casing, epitaphs. . . .
Howl, jet, and be damned, like a soul left over
No one believes in.
                    Leave me alone,

It's nearly dawn. I'll have coffee and go down there,
Down where the cropped skulls gaze and turn to stone
Blue Angels mow the grass with their afterburners
And the mind can rest in violence.
                    I am calm,
Pre-set, locked, and men like me go far,
Farther than anyone thinks and farthest in dreams.
Angels in thousands track me on a scope,
Drop me through sleep, leap me in release
Through parting cloud, a missile bound and free
Outpacing the flight of time in an upward thrust.

The men are all dead who sent me on my way:
Now accelerators, archers of the arrow of time,
Feather the flowing shaft with men like me
To mind the missile steady as she goes
Outward to her end where that may fall.

The jets go star- and seaward now in waves,
Squadron and wing like the future obsolete,
Sheathed in new vectors yet all past inside,
I feel them cling to height.
                    Angels ten thousand,
Thirty thousand and the target clear:
Release me, curve me downwards, falling free
Out of this towering sphere of time on fire
Into the old world—water, earth and air.

                                        Louis Coxe

A LETTER

Looking out of the dark of the town
At midnight, looking down
Into water under the lighthouse:
Abstractedly, timelessly looking
For something beneath the jetty,
Waiting for the dazed, silent flash,

Like the painless explosion that kills one,
To come from above and slide over
And empty the surface for miles—
The useless, imperial sweep
Of utter light—you see
A thicket of little fish

Below the squared stone of your window,
Catching, as it passes,
The blue afterthought of the blaze.
Shone almost into full being,
Inlaid in frail gold in their floor,
Their collected vision sways

Like dust among them;
You can see the essential spark
Of sight, of intuition,
Travel from eye to eye.
The next leg of light that comes round
Shows nothing where they have been,

But words light up in the head
To take their deep place in the darkness,
Arcing quickly from image to image
Like mica catching the sun:
The words of a love letter,
Of a letter to a long-dead father,

To an unborn son, to a woman
Long another man's wife, to her children,
To anyone out of reach, not born,
Or dead, who lives again,
Is born, is young, is the same:
Anyone who can wait no longer

Beneath the huge blackness of time
Which lies concealing, concealing
What must gleam forth in the end,
Glimpsed, unchanging, and gone
When memory stands without sleep
And gets its strange spark from the world.

JAMES DICKEY

ARMOR

When this is the thing you put on
The world is pieced slowly together
In the power of the crab and the insect.
The make of the eyeball changes
As over your mouth you draw down
A bird's bill made for a man.

As your weight upon earth is redoubled
There is no way of standing alone
More, or no way of being
More with the bound, shining dead.
You have put on what you should wear,
Not into the rattling of battle,

But into a silence where nothing
Threatens but Place itself: the shade
Of the forest, the strange, crowned
Motionless sunlight of Heaven,
With the redbird blinking and shooting
Across the nailed beam of the eyepiece.

In that light, in the wood, in armor,
I look in myself for the being
I was in a life before life
In a glade more silent than breathing,
Where I took off my body of metal
Like a brother whose features I knew

By the feel of their strength on my face
And whose limbs by the shining of mine.
In a vision I fasten him there,
The bright locust shell of my strength
Like a hanged man waiting in Heaven,
And then steal off to my life.

In my home, a night nearer death,
I wake with no shield on my breastbone,
Breathing deep through my sides like an insect,
My closed hand falling and rising
Where it lies like the dead on my heart.
I cannot remember my brother;

Before I was born he went from me
Ablaze with the meaning of typhoid.
In a fever I see him turn slowly
Under the strange, perfect branches
Where somehow I left him to wait
That I might be naked on earth,

His crowned face dazzlingly closed,
His curving limbs giving off
Pure energy into the leaves.
When I give up my hold on my breath
I long to dress deeply at last
In the gold of my waiting brother

Who shall wake and shine on my limbs
As I walk, made whole, into Heaven.
I shall not remember his face
Or my dazed, eternal one
Until I have opened my hand
And touched the grave glow of his breast

To stop the gaunt turning of metal:
Until I have let the still sun
Down into the stare of the eyepiece
And raised its bird's beak to confront
What man is within to live with me
When I begin living forever.

JAMES DICKEY

BY CANOE THROUGH THE FIR FOREST

Into the slain tons of needles,
On something like time and dark knowledge
That cannot be told, we are riding
Over white stones, forward through fir trees,
Following whatever the river
Through the clasping of roots follows deeply.

As we go inward, more trunks
Climb from the edge of the water
And turn on the banks and stand growing.
The nerves, in the patches of tree-light
On the ripples, can feel no death,
But shake like the wings of angels

With light hard pressed to keep up,
Though it is in place on each feather.
Heavy woods in one movement around us
Flow back along either side,
Bringing in more essential curves;
Small stones in their thousands turn corners

Under water and bear us on
Through the glittering, surfacing wingbeats
Cast from above. As we pass over,
As we pass through each hover of gold,
We lift up our blades from the water,
And the blades of our shoulders,

Our rowing muscles, our wings,
Are still and tremble, undying,
Drifting deeper into the forest.
Each light comes into our life
Past the man in front's changed hair,
Then along the wing-balancing floor,

And then onto me and one eye,
And into my mouth for an instant.
The stones beneath us grow rounder
As I taste the fretted light fall
Through living needles to be here
Like a word I can feed on forever,

Or believe like a vision I have
Or want to conceive out of greenness.
While the world fades, it is *becoming*.
As trees shut away all seeing,
In my mouth I mix it with sunlight.
Here, in the dark, it is *being*.

JAMES DICKEY

THE DUSK OF HORSES

Right under their noses, the green
Of the field is paling away
Because of something fallen from the sky.

They see this, and put down
Their long heads deeper in grass
That only just escapes reflecting them

As the dream of a millpond would.
The color green flees over the grass
Like an insect, following the red sun over

The next hill. The grass is white.
There is no cloud so dark and white at once;
There is no pool at dawn that deepens

Their faces and thirsts as this does.
Now they are feeding on solid
Cloud, and, one by one,

With nails as silent as stars among the wood
Hewed down years ago and now rotten,
The stalls are put up around them.

Now if they lean, they come
On wood on any side. Not touching it, they sleep.
No beast ever lived who understood

What happened among the sun's fields,
Or cared why the color of grass
Fled over the hill while he stumbled,

Led by the halter to sleep
On his four taxed, worthy legs.
Each thinks he awakens where

The sun is black on the rooftop,
That the green is dancing in the next pasture,
And that the way to sleep

In a cloud, or in a risen lake,
Is to walk as though he were still
In the drained field standing, head down,

To pretend to sleep when led,
And thus to go under the ancient white
Of the meadow, as green goes

And whiteness comes up through his face
Holding stars and rotten rafters,
Quiet, fragrant, and relieved.

JAMES DICKEY

AT BEDTIME

Near the bespoken animals, your face,
Wide, before words, with its unknowing smile,
Asks of me at your bedside, yet a while
Not to reflect.

          With the reflection, grace
Manifests, and the wound demands the side.
Animals stare uncomprehendingly;
We talk together, and are crucified.

Bent by intelligent language in your blood,
That from your nature into knowledge burns,
You must reach out to that intolerant good
Strapped on the cross. It is what language learns.

Your face, at night, sleeping, beyond all harms,
With the endearing animals is entire,
Yet it will wake not to their nursing arms,
But to blind fire.

Talk to me, talk, engage: we are of God's
Most terrible gesture the inheritor,
That speech made flesh that stumbles in our blood,
That red voice of our holy creditor.

Talk to me, talk. Men in the burst of day,
Their mouths pried open by that ghost's return,
Will speak such words as are intent to flay
The flesh from bone, and mind from body burn.

There is no tongue for animals to speak,
Nor sacrament forces their shallow eye,
But a clear flesh they linger at your feet,
Done and put by.

You, toward the night, young beyond speaking, stay
With these bespoken animals of your heart,
But will fall helpless down the cliff of day
When in your flesh the speaking senses start,

And under pain and under fear of pain
Will loose the animal languor from your tongue,
When what your innocence cannot restrain
Sings your own song.

I to you nothing yet, not law, not voice,
Not prophesier of the wounded side,
A shadow on the lamplight, a bent noise,
A filled place at your ritual bedside,

I will speak for you for another night,
Sponsor and cannibal, your blackened friend,
Oldest of your possessions and most light,
That nightly strokes your hair, to his own end.

But in some morning you will understand
Each goes to each, each lies in his own place.
Then, as the door devours you, turn and send
To the animals that last light of your face.

WILLIAM DICKEY

NOT THIS

What I intended was not this
Grey absence when the heart declines
Like a spent flower upon its stalk,

The bent, the reprimanded head.

What I intended was to say
Not in all things perfection lies,
Nor are our human reasons pure—

But you set out, as from some shore
Obsidian-sharp, at once to sea,
Where the most drowning waters are.

It was not meant so finally.

Meant as a thesis, not yet proved,
A speculation, hardly said,
The merest whisper of a voice—

But at the sound you bowed your head.
The universal darkness fell,
The landscape shattered to a close.
The frozen eyes of hell arose
And glittered where the stars had been.
Calamity undid the moon.

What I intended was not this.

Think of those words as wholly gone,
Think of the rush of summer sun
Where man stands warmly perfected—

Of me not thinking things again.

WILLIAM DICKEY

CALYPSO

This was mortal reasoning beyond her understanding.
She offered him the god-gift, promised him
Immortality if he would marry her:
Yet behold him, undecided, even sceptical,
Pacing the vine-hung seaward terrace,
His fingers teasing the harshness of his beard,
Begging time to consider, time to weigh his answer.

Time! Ye gods! Time to consider
The god-gift, the blazon of immortality!
Was she not beautiful? Was she not young,
High-breasted and not given to boisterousness?
Was this not matchless dowry for heroic man?

She sought in thonged sandals to match his stride:
Her eyes sought the focus of his seaward gaze,
Swinging above vine and orchard of fig
To where the light lay brazen, broken on the sea—
Brazen as orient bangle at her wrist.
Beauty, youth; and immortality to enjoy;
Yet something ponderous, treacherous in his tread.
How understand this mortal calculation?

Scars of journeys those scorings at his eyes,
Season on season, sealight and sun of ceaseless seasons,
And his mouth moist with juice of fig, his beard
Streaked with the bleaching of an ocean's weather.
Turning as he turned in the vine-wedged light
She heard him mutter on the thought of time;
A voyage through a circling calendar of seasons.
It was less than she expected, much less than she hoped:
Greek complaint and Greek suspicion of her promise.

And all the while his hands, calloused from sword-hilt,
Chafed and hardened from the long haul of a journey,
Evaded the olive promise of her island flesh.
Sated with nymph and immortal goddess
His eyes held long the brass light of the sea.

Songs of a fading war, fading songs, a journey:
What were the songs his mouth remembered?
Time? There had been time enough.
Immortal enjoyment of beauty and youth?
The years, the seasons etching his face
Had taught him soon love's quick mortality.
Forever upon this island was too long
By some many indolent, kissing lifetimes.
Yet she was young, beautiful, high-breasted;
Sang to his plucking like a tautened lyre,
Paced short with him here upon the terrace,
Flesh laved with running shadow, dappled in light,
Turning and turning as the sealight burned,
Hair dark as midnight in her midnight cave.

Nostalgia was it? It must be more
Driving him in the direction of his destiny,
Launched again on waters of a god-wrecked voyage.
From brazen sealight his hard hand rose;
On seaward terrace brazen bangle gleamed:
Marbled, olive flesh dappled with leaves' light,
Bronze sail filling splashed with sealight,
Veined with trembling light. Under the vine, and distant,
The tears stubbornly falling, the cry forming.

Refusing her gift he left her these tokens.
These Greek and independent children.
His boat beat seaward now, heeling
To her parting gift of sailing weather,

The breeze moving alder and cypress,
Wafting smoke from the cedar-wood island fires,
Troubling the unbound, dark and wondrous hair.
Cloaked in stuff of bronze and gold,
His head turned toward the horizon—
He whom she had rescued solitary from the sea.
Five years she had lain with him, nymph and bride,
To lose him seaward now against the light:
Her own hands had provisioned the boat
Whose great oar opened now its wash,
Fan of distance, wedge of his going,
That wake in whose wake she gently mourned.
Until he was lost, afloat in distance,
Bearing his mortality like a god.

MAURICE DUGGAN

SOME, NOT ALL

Women have loved bulls and swans,
God in the form of a golden shower.
Now machines stamp out both swan and bull
And one can shake an aura from a box.
But something in the meretricious present tense
May indeed protect the beautiful—
Those persistent dreamers and their swan necks
Will rut somehow and hide their power:
Mothers, lacking vows, get along on tricks.

I have known one or two who slept with god,
Caught them looking down along some pool,
Or drenched in sunlight's spiritual seed.
One who followed hoofprints in the mud
Seemed, of all, perhaps, in purest need
And certainly, to me, not cynical.
They would have thought themselves depraved
To pose as innocent or fool
And never once ally themselves with what
    the body craved.

When it was over and done with, one said,
Sprinkled with gold, bruised and beaked,
I am an ordinary woman and would have stayed
So if I had not been harshly used.
The swan retreating, the bull running, thus
Took on the look of those who were refused.
She had no trouble trading sensual death
When Minos, Castor, Pollux, Perseus,
Would bulge and struggle in the womb of myth.

                CHARLES EDWARD EATON

DIRGE FOR HILDA DOOLITTLE

What garlands shall we bring,
Persephone,
what offering
to honor her who loved
"Greek flower, Greek ecstasy?"

Bring cypress boughs
and sheaves
of mist-grey olive leaves.
Come with cornel buds
—white spray on spray—
and coronals of bay.

Bring saxifrage
that cleaves
the rocks
      —and shocks
of red anemones.
                Bring these:
pale mountain cyclamens
among their silver-veined,
thick leaves.

Come with clematis
and wreaths
      of citron leaf.
Bring hyacinths
—dark, curly-headed hyacinths—
sprung from Apollo's grief.

Come with violets
—purple, white, Aegean-blue—

Illyrian violets
she sang and praised so well.
Bring asphodel,
blue rosemary and rue.

Come bearing poppies, too,
for her repose—
and, as a token of her song,
entwine wild vine
                    with one sea rose.

MICHEL FARANO

DOLPHIN

In mythology the restraint shown by dolphins
Is praiseworthy. Foregoing the preposterous they are
Content with only a little more than
Truth. They do what actual-factual dolphins
Have been known to do in times
Past or times present: pilot a ship
Or ride a small boy bareback smiling.

Conversely real dolphins seem influenced by myth
As if the overheard story of Arion
Could furnish endless inspiration in a dolphin's
Daily life. Such was Opo of Opononi,
Opo of the Antipodes, Opo who let
Non-dolphin fellow-bathers stroke his back.
And when he died New Zealand mourned.

Having achieved, after how many ages, dry
Land, these beasts returned to live successfully
With sharks and devilfish. Having achieved dry
Land they achieved the sea. And this
Was long long before the first myth.
Today the uninhabitable for us, thank Dolphin,
Is that much less uninhabitable and inhospitable.

In weather foggy-shaggy in mid-Atlantic
Watching their water-sports, tumbling, leap-frog
Who could be wholly in the doldrums
Doleful? A rough sea chuckles with dolphins
And a smooth sea dimples. Delft-blue.
Delphinium-blue blooming with white morning-glories.
The sea relaxes. They tickle the sea.

Love Conquered by a Dolphin could equally
Be called A Dolphin Conquered by Love.
The sea-beast holds the god coiled
But his moony upward-rolling eyes tell
Who is the more hopelessly caught. Preposterous?
The antique sculptor shrugs: with so ravishing
A god what could poor dolphin do?

From the large brain intricate as man's
And slightly larger one could predict intelligence
And from intelligence superior to a dog's,
An ape's, an elephant's, one could predict
Language, but where is science to predict
 (Much less explain) benevolence such as Opo's,
Opo riding a small boy bareback smiling?

Nothing less than forgiveness dolphins teach us
If we, miraculously, let ourselves be taught.
Enduring scientific torture no dolphin has yet
 (With experimental electrodes hammered into its skull)
In righteous wrath turned on its tormentors.
What will science ever find more precious?
The sea relaxes. They bless the sea.

Robert Francis

THOREAU IN ITALY

Lingo of birds was easier than the lingo of peasants.
They were elusive, though, the birds, for excellent reasons.
He thought of Virgil, Virgil who wasn't there to chat with.

History he never forgave for letting Latin
lapse into Italian, a renegade jabbering
musical enough but not enough to call music.

So he conversed with stones, imperial and papal.
Even the preposterous popes he could condone
a moment for the clean arrogance of their inscriptions.

He asked the Italians only to leave him in the past
alone, but this was what they emphatically never did.
Being the present, they never ceased to celebrate it.

Something was always brushing him on the street, satyr
or saint—impossible to say which the more foreign.
At home he was called touchy; here he knew he was.

Impossible to say. The dazzling nude with sex
lovingly displayed like carven fruit, the black
robe sweeping a holy and unholy dust.

Always the flesh whether to lacerate or kiss—
conspiracy of fauns and clerics smiling back
and forth at each other acquiescently through leaves.

Caught between wan monastic mountains wearing the
    tonsure
and the all-siren, ever-dimpling sea, he saw—
how could he fail?—at heart geography to blame.

So home to Concord where (as he might have known he
    would)
he found the Italy he wanted to remember.
Why had he sailed if not for the savour of returning?

An Italy distilled of all extreme, conflict,
collusion—an Italy without the Italians—
in whose green context he could con again his Virgil.

In cedar he read cypress, in the wild apple, olive.
His hills would stand up favourably to the hills of Rome.
His arrowheads could hold their own with art Etruscan.

And Walden clearly was his Mediterranean
whose infinite colors were his picture-gallery.
How far his little boat transported him—how far.

Robert Francis

NOTE ON THE ILIAD

Why are epics
always about
the anti-life
of a noble lout?

I sing Lely
who burnt no tower
but brought the sea-floor
into flower.

Imagine it—
the moment when
out of the
architectured fen

the polder surfaced
sleek as a whale
and still awash.
Then the last veil

of standing water
slides away.
Glistening land
like a wet tray

serves up its past,
wreck upon wreck
glazed in the sand
of this smooth deck:

like Ararat,
the antique shores
ride up again
ready for Noahs.

Now wheat ripples
where schooner and barque
thrashed down the waters
to ultimate dark—

avenued Holland
waves over plains
which twenty years back
rocked fishing-seines.

Hard to imagine
the North Sea floor
was where we picnic—
and even more

to imagine this:
a people at grips
with genesis
not apocalypse.

        RAYMOND GARLICK

BLACK VULTURES OVER GUAYMAS

Harbor: The hissing whistle of their wings dividing the light
Above the red islands often lifted my head;
And the sky, filled with the purpose of a hundred hurrying vultures,
Interpreted the sea, rustling its different sibilants.

Town: I felt a spell of blue sharpen the thorns of the earth;
I heard the active town coursing its labyrinth
Of bisque about the harbor and backward amid the hills
Lie still, a mast of shell abandoned to the sun.

Cemetery: And, past the last sharp shack and barefoot paths, I saw
Walled-in dead monuments bedizened with awful love,
Paper blossoms of fear and trivia of doubt.
Then in my empty hand I read the palm of dust.

Desert: Over all frozen eyes, the black doves of that waste
Passed to its ashen edge where their consuming peace
Became those distances, westward the ocean plain,
Landward a sea of light, the opal stare of haze—

Garden: Calcine of rose, old ash, quick with Arabian flame:
A line of egrets wavering eastward over the waves,

A whitewing dove in the dove-loud green of a
 carob bough
Over the hearts of the living, who listen and heed
 the tree.

Brewster Ghiselin

THE BODY'S INDEPENDENCE

I

Father Bianchi taught biology
in Bombay's Don Bosco High School, but skipped
the parts I had learnt about already.
The classroom beamed faces, keen and tight-lipped,
bare brown arms on desks, fingers steady.

His white cassock arm-sleeves rolled against heat,
the Father went through the motions of the body
with a cane to point at a chart and hit
on our heads. His voice, a lesson in prosody,
told us of the secrets of the heart.

He demonstrated man, the button at his throat
loose: he described in the air, with his cane,
the nervous system, showed how the brain was alert.
We furtively laughed at the shape of man,
but his eyes saw further than the chart.

II

A hawk stood high above Malabar Hill,
watching the whole island. In the afternoon's
sun-stunned silence a coconut fell.
A dog, his skin vibrating over bones
to rid him of flies, barked. And I fell ill:

kidney haemorrhage that oozed blood
into the bladder. I felt the hawk's beak
pull at a kidney, like a worm out of mud,
as my skin shrank and tightened over the weak
skeleton. All the pains the heart withstood,

and did not fall. A kind woman by my bed
kept vigil, telling a favourite tale:
how Babur, the Mogul King, prayed and tried
to bring back his son to life and grew pale
himself with Humayun's illness and died.

But Humayun had lived to rule. She said
a whole kingdom waited to see me crowned,
with the oil of life to anoint my head.
My body took shape like the chart, I found
the outline of bones fill with flesh and blood.

III

A crow shifted from his nest to a branch,
pulled his black tongue at the sun and let fall
a splotch of white into the shade. A finch
flew out. The crow laughed. An eagle, appalled,
moved to another tree. A snake looked, flinched.

India was at civil war,
the crow excreted where he pleased. And I,
reborn from a fairy-tale, saw bones charred
in mounds on pavements. It was no country
for princes, and the eagle soared

above the darker clouds. The undergrowth
heaved uneasily with poison of snakes.
'The heart is free!' people cried. 'What if truth
runs out like blood? We have our independence.'
The blood of India ran out with my youth.

ZULFIKAR GHOSE

SAETAS DE DOLORES

She came her thousand miles
for life and died while I
prayed in my frozen town.
What's a telephone to bring
that lie looping
down the miles of north?
I thanked whoever
told me death
as prisoners thanked once
their executioners
then fell
on me to claw
me from that blood to light.

Her heart hurt
grew twice life size
it beat so big
it shook the bed we lay in
when she stayed with me.
That heart exploded
shakes me still though she turns
easy with her well-lost world.

They boxed her body
shipped iridescent shell
west of my silence
so I never saw her dead
yet if I set her bright
bones at my ear she would
Christ sing.

Her neck where my hand
rested once and her stark
bones I should have kissed.

Dry winds swoop on me from home
to tell how they diminish
in the high
sweet desert.

Give me one
bone carpal
of the left hand
anything
a spear
to lance me
of that sere
grass growing
out of her
breast and the dark
night of her
emptied eyes.

        SUZANNE GROSS

IN THE KITCHEN OF THE OLD HOUSE

    In the kitchen of the old house, late,
I was making some coffee
    and I day-dreamed sleepily of old friends.
Then the dream turned. I waited.
    I walked alone all day in the town
where I was born. It was cold,
    a Saturday in January
when nothing happens. The streets
    changed as the sky grew dark around me.
The lamps in the small houses
    had tassels on them, and the black cars
at the curb were old and square.
    A ragman passed with his horse, their breaths
blooming like white peonies,
    when I turned into a darker street
and I recognized the house
    from snapshots. I felt as separate
as if the city and the house
    were closed inside a globe which I shook
to make it snow. No sooner
    did I think of snow, but snow started
to fill the heavy darkness
    around me. It reflected the glare
of the streetlight as it fell
    melting on the warmth of the sidewalk
and frozen on frozen grass.
    Then I heard out of the dark the sound
of steps on the bare cement
    in a familiar rhythm. Under
the streetlight, bent to the snow,
    hatless, younger than I, so young that
I was not born, my father
    walked home to his bride and his supper.

A shout gathered inside me
   like a cold wind, to break the rhythm,
to keep him from entering
   that heavy door—but I stood under
a tree, closed in by the snow,
   and did not shout, to tell what happened
in twenty years, in winter,
   when his early death grew inside him
like snow piling on the grass.
   He opened the door and met the young
woman who waited for him.

                        Donald Hall

A POET IN NEED

A poet in need of a bed, having the price of a bed
Approached an hotel:
'Have you a single or preferably a double—
In case I pick up a friend—
Room for the night?' 'Certainly sir'
Replied the reception desk
'Please write your name and occupation
Here in this book.'
'Name Laureate Skellykeats profession Poet.'
He wrote. 'Sorry sir,' said the reception desk
'We have no accommodation for poets.
They seldom pay.'

'So what am I to do?' said the poet.
'Sorry sir,' said the reception desk,
But, being a humane object, it leaned over and whispered:
'Try two doors down the road.
They like poets there.'

Two doors down the road was the advertising agency.
It embraced him with its octopus arms:
'We love poets here. Come in.
Poets work for us. They write
Memorable slogans. Come in
And join the night-shift.'

'But I don't want to work,' said the poet
'I simply want to sleep.' 'Try two doors down the road.
Anyone can sleep there.'

Two doors down the road was the entrance to the cemetery:
'I want a bed,' said the poet
'Single, double or intermediate.
I am a poet.' 'Sorry sir,' said
The paid and grizzled cemetery-keeper,
'We don't have poets here.'
'Why not?' said the poet, 'Everyone else
Can sleep here.' 'No,' said the keeper.
'Why not, please tell me why not?'
'The neighbours would complain.
We can't have all these corpses get up and dance.'

                      JOHN HEATH-STUBBS

THE WAR MUSEUM AT NAGASAKI

Here are two helmets, stamped
With the marks of burning death:
A twisted toy in a case
The lid marked by the breath
Of a passer-by;
Smudged in the photograph
A dying patient's face
Smiling patiently;
Where the sorrow tramped
He holds a bitter staff.

A woman pauses now
Fixing her hat in the glass,
Squinting to read the words
That summon up the crass
Immoment, silly facts:
The dates of birth and dying,
Name, height, the broken sherds
Of long-dead artefacts;
Broken is that bough,
The rest is useless lying.

Our pity, *their* regret
Are lost before the face
Of truth, the hollow bowl,
The twisted worthless trace
Of broken wedding rings.
Nothing, nothing can work,
Not love nor pity, yet
One registers those things,
Throwing the dead a net
Across that foundering dark.

CHARLES HIGHAM

EDWARD HICKS'S OLD PICTURE

The lion does not lie down with the lamb, no.
The paw at the end of his mind slashes once,
And a small life bloodies the peaceable kingdom,
But not enough smear to cover the difference.
Where lion is, a curly woolen lamb is dead.
My children are furies, but not kin playmates
To sliding adders, or tiger with the big head.

I had seven goldfish once that could not read,
And rode a horse, rich-coated, biddable, fast,
But a horse. They taught me my counter-fable.
I kept a seagull fed for weeks, but felt nearest
When it was seagull most, and flew away.
I imagined myself into the real life of cat,
Pig, and pup, for a small part of any day.

I knew a woman like a leopard, supple and striped,
And lay down with her, skin to skin. She tore
The thinking off my ribs, cloud out of my eyes.
I knew a shambler once, a man like a grizzly bear,
Awkward on his hind feet, a Brutus under the hat.
I had also for teacher a gaudy parrot or loon
I thought of awhile as a woman, but stopped that.

If a lynx in my fable has his arm round my lamb,
I shoot, to kill. Or windmill at him with a club,
In a game of beating his bones into the ground.
Nor does my fable say people are animals curbed.
I teach the children that people are women
      and men
Whose blue eyes and warm hands, whose voices,
Brains, and sex, can kill, they cannot guess when.

The old obsessed painter turned me foolish, too,
The damnation of being left to myself by a liar,
Till my hands remembered the woman was
    woman-smooth,
That after the heavy-overcoated man I was poor.
I comfortable have not known till late I am
Not in a war. I am a war of love and unlove.
And how no lion ever lay down with a lamb.

JOHN HOLMES

FAITHFUL READER

I'd rather read stories that end before I want them to,
Than long, long stories I don't want to finish but should
Before I begin the next—which might be one that ends
Without my hearing the red-headed girl whose wit I like
Speak her wild mind out—or might be another long one.

I read about a wronged husband who boiled his black-hearted
Wife's betrayer down to the bones, an artist in a limited way,
But why get to it years later, around page five hundred fifty?
I knew one preacher with terminal facilities, but only one.

All my visitors overstay an hour, and when I go to call,
Even on the most famous man I know, I catch myself wishing
To have been there. Music backs up one measure, goes two.

Funerals and weddings are over before the principals know it,
And with or without words, love-making makes its own end.

And a story is a story as long as there are new happenings.

Inaugurals and college commencements would never get raves
On the drama page, it takes so long to lose new characters
In the old plot, and there are too many, many, speaking parts.
I'm in a hurry for new action, not in westerns. In easterns.
Hungry like the end of the world and all the stores closed.
But even if I had forever, I'd break it up and out of there,
To the library for a one-week book, and finish it before bed,
Chewing and talking, the music on, the family in and out.

JOHN HOLMES

THE YOUNG GIRL AT THE BALL

While the young girl, with her full breasts and thighs
Eloquent through her clothes, moves as a tree
Bends and returns against the torrents of air,
The voice of my Demon falters, the babble dies
Around me; and, as the music ends, I see
Her smile and watch her walking back to her chair.

When I was young I should have found in her arms
My venture, my voyage, the talisman and the sign,
Had I straddled her beautiful flanks or gathered her
    breast in my hand.
Each turn of the fabulous way would be quick with
    alarms
Where the dreadful crags thrust up through their
    forests of pine
And the dragons stirred in their dens as I rode through
    that land.

Had I been older, I should have entered her gate
As a traveller coming home to the cherished fire
Of a house where the heart goes in and out at its need;
I should have learned to move to her music, to wait
Through all the returning seasons of desire
For ripeness, and seen her belly abundant with my seed.

I have journeyed; I have come home; it is late in the
    year to depart.
She will not move to my arms or come to my bed.
She turns and smiles into other eyes than mine.
What is it, then, tears at my animal heart?
As I watched her dance, in every gesture I read
The challenge, the summons, the unmistakable sign

Of the sensual miracle: Now, at last, I see
Those hidden presences and powers, aware
Of a promise kept, of mysteries revealed;
Just as the eye observes from the motions of the tree
All the invisible energies of the air
In the toss and recoil of boughs in an open field.

A. D. Hope

Melbourne, 1955

NEWS FROM THE CITY

If ever again you should come to our problematic
Dust-devilled, memory-pestered city
You would find nothing changed. At noon the sullen
Flag still hangs heavy, close to the masthead,
Despite the riots and tornadoes.
                           Still on the ramparts
The sentry paces and looks out seaward
Over the bright ennui of the new quarter.
Even the names of streets were left unaltered
After the last coup;
            and they still hold
The same population of pimps and hawkers,
The old fears and unkept promises.
Along the grand boulevards
                        the same cripples and beggars
Stare nobly through ruined eyeballs,
Search dustbins for cheese-rinds and diamonds.
O and on summer mornings the same explosions
Of green and gold from roadside trees; in the parks
The same booby-traps of desire and joy.

You remember the outbreak of girls with quattrocento
Cheekbones, the doe-eyed children dropped from an angel
    choir?

You could reconstitute all the old habits—
Hide in the cinema through long afternoons,
Light a candle before the Black Virgin,
Wait once more for the lotteries that never pay.
You could sit (with me, if you liked) on the stone bench
Under the castle wall,
Look over tawny acres of tile and brick-dust,
And still be sure as ever that somewhere among them
You must find some day a roof, your roof, to shelter
The dream the film offered and the candle paid for.

Winters are still hard and summers torrid.
Your health needed a change; and since you left
To live abroad in a less irrational climate,
Without crippling diseases or circular storms,
Doubtless our dooms and fallacies touch you no longer.
Yet there is always, they say, the urge to come back.

So various still in our city
The bargains on stalls in the markets, or promised
From wayside pulpits, so alluring the prizes
That fall to friends of geheimrats, or the respected
Ex-lovers of bawdy-house madams. It is so frequent
To hear of tiaras found lying on ash-heaps.
It would please me to see you again.
       For myself I shall stay here.

        GRAHAM HOUGH

THOSE TWO

1. EVE TO SATAN

Ah, I've learned: the shining fold, the summer,
Yourself like a fan astride a seamless pool,
My lover, my chance—they were all illusions.
I cherish them for that and forgive you,
But wish you had not withheld what you must have known:
Our timid tongues bruising the fruit's surface
Could only fling our pieces upon an unleaving bush.
Did you keep the core? Does it hang like a trophy
In some crevice of Hell, visited by the lonely?
For we should have gnawed that apple to its root
And the root itself, though raging in the throat,
Should have become our sense, all the way down.

Am I right? That apple swallowed whole,
The garden challenged, not a stem remaining,
All within ourselves, bitten as a lover bites,
That his lips recall the utter taste of time?

2. SATAN TO EVE

Vous avez raison. But your tone is wrong,
Nearly petulant, as though you spoke with your mouth full.
Swallow, girl, swallow!
Oh. I'm sorry: old ironies invite fresh mockeries.
But I, too, am disbarred from jolly Eden.
For when you ate an axe sprang from the sun
And split my snake to sorrow. The garden waits there,
Dusty, unvisited, no living thing about,
Though sometimes from my perch outside I see stirrings,
Motes of a feeble light seeking a mirror,

Bones of a hand fumbling for the glove of flesh.
No . . . the core remains, rotting upon the bush
Where you threw it; the ants are lugging it away,
Piecemeal, undiscoverable, like us, deceived.

Dear Eve, had you swallowed heaven with a gulp,
Even now, we would be dancing on the greensward,
Our bodies attuned to any bird that flies,
And I, like a knight come forth to his first adventure,
Would kneel to kiss your hand before the dazzling tourney.

DANIEL HUGHES

SUGAR-LOAF

The trickle cutting from the hill-crown
Whorls to a pure pool here, with a whisp trout like
    a spirit.
The water is wild as alcohol—
Distilling from the fibers of the blue wind.
Reeds, nude and tufted, shiver as they wade.

I see the whole huge hill in the small pool's stomach.

This will be serious for the hill.
It suspects nothing.
Crammed with darkness, the dull, trusting giant
Leans, as over a crystal, over the water
Where his future is forming.

                        TED HUGHES

FROM: THE FOURTH HOUR

What little vegetable is the favorite of the Christ Child?
Oh the Onion! Because it shows by sound how flesh was born
    and concentric are the rings of the stars that move
    around the sun.
Oh the onion, because it says how the human dies to his old
    skins one by one each one more new!

What little vegetable is the favorite of the Christ Child?
Oh the Apple! Because its skin is bloodred and its flesh
    snowwhite, oh the motherhood of flesh rolling in her bold
    red man, oh the apple because it shows the soul and spirit
    one—oh the apple, its seeds are star kingdoms!
Oh the Apple, because its humps are like a valentine's and a
    camel's.

What little vegetable is the favorite of the Christ Child?
Oh the Orange! Because in fire's orange kingdom no juicebody
    is alone but curled like a nest of unburnable
    puppydogs within the sun's secret, it is the identical many
    making one merry wheel, and oh the Orange its
    butterthick shineskin! You could never guess how many
    are inside without being one!

Which little vegetable is the favorite of the Christ Child?
Oh the Onion is Morning and the Apple Noon, and Orange
He burns all night in the Centre of the Earth.
I'm glad there are just three hours in the day.

White is the flesh of Christ and red His blood and orange is His
    gold heart.
Oh I love the egg in the yolk, I love its white flesh and I love its
    fragile shell.

Which little egg is the favorite of the Christ Child?
I love them all, I love all the hours in the day, especially when
 they happen instantly, all at once!
Oh substances within substances, oh vegetable eggs that give
 birth to three gold oranges:
 Snowwhite, Rosered, rolling down the mountain went
 three golden apples.
 Up the glass mountain on horseback goes the prince.
 This is the only time by the pomegranate. This is the one
 hour,
 this is the whole clock.
 It strikes in a twinkling!
        And all the witches croak!

Which little witch is the favorite of the Christ Child?
 Oh boogies on broomsticks, who has time to sweeten our
 lies for you! All the angels are busy truthing.
 Oh skyward princess in disguise, you know how lonely it
 would be with nobody to play scare with me!

Which little kingdom is the favorite of the Christ Child?
 Oh the *Children!*
 Imagining play!

              Kay Johnson

BY THE RIVERSIDE

Do not call from memory—all numbers have changed.
—From the cover of the Telephone Directory.

Once I lived at a Riverside
1-3-7-5, by a real stream, Hangman's Creek,
Named from an old pine, down the hill
On which three Indians died. As a child,
I modelled the Crucifixion on that tree
Because I'd heard two Indians were thieves
Strung up by soldiers from Fort Wright in early days,
But no one remembered who the third one was.

Once, in winter, I saw an old Indian wade,
Breaking the thin ice with his thighs.
His squaw crouched modestly in the water,
But he stood up tall, buck-naked. "Cold!" he said,
Proud of his iron flesh, the color of rust,
And his bold manhood, roused by the shock of ice.
He grinned as he spoke, struck his hard chest a blow
Once, with his fist . . . So I call, from memory,
That tall old Indian, standing in the water.

And I am not put off by an operator
Saying, "Sor-ree, the lion is busy . . ."
Then, I would tremble, seeing a real lion
Trammeled in endless, golden coils of wire,
Pawing a switchboard in some mysterious
Central office, where animals ran the world,
As I knew they did. To the brave belonged the power.
Christ was a brave, beneath that gauzy clout.

I whispered to the corners of my room, where lions
Crowded at night, blotting the walls with shadows,
As the wind tore at a gutter beneath the eaves,
Moaned with the power of quiet animals
And the old pine, down the hill, where Indians hung:
Telling my prayers, not on a pale-faced Sunday
Nor to a red God, who could walk on water
When winter hardened, and the ice grew stronger.

Now I call up god-head and manhood, both,
As they emerged for a child by the Riverside.
But they are all dead Indians now. They answer
Only to me. The numbers have not changed.

Carolyn Kizer

LOVEMUSIC

Come, freighted heart, within this port.
Bring all your bee-collected sweet,
The savor of a liberal night,
The crown of columbine, still wet,
The muse of days. Bring your delight
To fill the palate and the plate,
To rinse the lips. Unburden, set
Your lilies on my chair of state.

Come, laden love, to this, my cave.
For here we soon may hide and move,
In havens play the courting dove,
And pace the newly-altered nave:
This vested place, this heart alive.
With wine and fruit and coupled favor
Each of the other's self to savor.

Come candidly, consort with me,
And spill our pleasure for a day.
Let love delay, unhurriedly,
This passing taste . . . I prophesy:
Remembered cinnamon and lime
Will fructify a bleaker time.

CAROLYN KIZER

SISYPHUS

When I was young and full of shame
I knew a legless man who came

inside a little cart, inchmeal,
flatirons on his hands, downhill.

Under the railroad bridge his chant
singsonged all day *repent, repent*

for Jesus. On the way to school
I spoke to him to save my soul

and coming back, he made me stop
to count the nickels in his cap.

Eyes level with my petticoat
he whined to me. I smelled his goat-

smell, randy, thick, as brown as blood.
I did the only thing I could.

I wheeled my master up the hill.
I rolled him up as he sat still.

Up past the sisters of Saint Joe
I pushed my stone so God would know.

And he, who could not genuflect
on seamy stumps, stitched his respect

with fingers in the air. He called
me a perfect Christian child.

One day I said I was a Jew.
I wished I had. I wanted to.

The basket man is gone; the stone
I push up hill is all my own.

MAXINE W. KUMIN

WITH OPEN LOVE

There was great purpose in our going down.
Harp, sackbut hardened
Shadrach, Meshach and Abednego
To sweep the salamander stream.
My Shadrach's eyes, bigger and darker, swifter,
Lit on the flitting beast that
Called, commanded us to come.
    Given the time on earth,
    He too would learn to walk.

Sounds of the cornet and the flute
Cracked from their salamander throats.
Cries of the psaltery water
Splashed to our crashing feet.
My Shadrach's hands, and Meshach's,
Stretched to the twisting beast
That culled, arrested us in flight.
    Given the time in water,
    He too would learn to swim.

There was great purpose in our going down.
Harp, sackbut softened
Shadrach, Meshach and Abednego
To loose their tightening grip.
My Meshach's voice, higher and stronger, swifter,
Cried for the fleeing beast,
That we not crush its tail.
    Given the time in air,
    He too would learn to breathe.

Barks of the cornets and the flutes
Blasted our eyes, our throats,
Tore at our wavering hands
As salamander slid beneath the mud.
Our blond Abednego, and Shadrach,
Saw that the twisting waters
Swirled, swept to flame.
               Given the time in fire,
                 He too would learn to live.

Strung dulcimer, strike the
Gold-image-bearing-king.
Hide, Salamander. Burn deep
The pristine chambers of the brain. But let our
Shadrach, Meshach and Abednego,
Go, go, with open love.
This is no dunghill, but our heart.
               Earth, water, air and fire,
               Be all. Be all as we.

                        KONSTANTINOS LARDAS

CLAUDIA GOODBYE

(From a Roman Epitaph)

Claudia the Roman hailed us from her grave.
*Stand, stranger, friend, and read me. What I say
is not much.* Pride shortens words to the way-
farer's haste, the desperate "traveller, stay"
is said with dignity. Remember me.
The tomb is nothing. I was beautiful.
Or it's the stone that spoke in letters. She
was lovely, not the monument, to see.
*Claudia was the name her parents gave.
She loved her husband in her heart,* it says,
deilexit, diligently, with delight
or what? And from such loving nights and days
together, *she gave birth
to two sons, one of whom she left on earth
and one beneath it* when she lost her light
(Cornelia with one dead jewel now).
Read on. *Pleasant to talk to, and her step was neat.*
Did I not tell you she was beautiful?
She was a housekeeper. She worked in wool.
And that is all, for *I have spoken. Go.*

She lives in letters, and the gravestone's art
pins down forever one time out of time,
and stops the squeeze of death that stopped
    the heart
so long as the eyes read, and the words chime,
and the brain loves the shape behind the rhyme,
and Psyche stirs in the embrace of butterflies
and eyes that were her eyes and are my eyes.

So, Claudia. And have you told us all?
You speak so well, and can you not recall
just some unlicensed moment from behind
    the grave?
We ask no confidence, but was there not some
    incomplete
time, sense of failure, moments not so neat
to gather to your basket, when that precious wool
was dead in the fingers, and the mind gone dull
and stale with ease and trying to contrive
some fact to want and want and not to have,
and the desire to want lost in the course
of state and matron's honors and the full
long dutiful and dedicated hours?
Speak, Claudia, speak.
                    But I have spoken. Call
no more.
        But was this all? Claudia, all?

I speak for her. I am the gravestone. I
tell you, good friend, in Claudia's name, goodbye.
Now give her leave to say: Leave me alone.
Your Claudia is written on the stone
for you to read. The rest is Claudia's own.

                RICHMOND LATTIMORE

OH THE COSSACKS

Where are the cossacks,
the horse raiders with sabres
sharp enough to cut God's beard
who would have whipped my father
all the way from Kiev to the Czar's war,
had he not chopped off his right, third finger
at the knuckle in one stroke?

Better to be maimed than a murderer,
he had whispered to the Rabbi
who had been stunned to unbelief
by the cleaver still bleeding furiously.
What has death to do with a Jew?

I would ask him that now
seeing his dead face
return in this repose to a clear happiness
I had not seen in it for years,
eyes lidded in a contemplation
of absolutes his life had moved too swiftly
from, as wind will sometimes chase
smoke from its fire to be dispersed
in the light air.

Here lies that man, expensively,
in one of his ten Sabbath suits,
his right hand holding down
his talked-out heart
as in some final oath,
the four remaining fingers
so fleshed with the gold moments
of the gold country he espoused
the third is not missed, seems merely

to be bent at the healed knuckle
and pointing inward at the heart
long since delivered from its cossack terror.

I would ask him now,
was it a Gentile angel
who tumbled him up in black nets
like the short-of-breath fish he had become?
I would ask him.

But he would laugh and lift both chins
saying: Forget this foolishness.
Go make a dollar. What are you boring for
into my ribs with your questions?
Who remembers Russia after all these years?
Cossacks were cossacks, a cholera take them.

Yes. I would ask him
but he is dead,
and in those last years
memory turned fat choking his understanding.
The finger he would rather lose
than curl around the barrel of a gun
is absent now, missed by no one.
But I, I might still ask him:
Where are the cossacks,
do they never ride?
Without the devils we give fingers for
can the Messiah come?

But he lives patriarchally composed,
well fed in death
as if to say: What cossacks?
Go make a dollar. Be something.

OSWALD LEWINTER

DAY OF DANCING

Within a quiet neighbourhood of huts
The rhythm starts, as if each builded branch
And thatch of leaves, from one tree caught and cut
By final winters of the axe, asserted
Together as a common circumstance
Their single sap and all the vanished birds
Which once were held at singing and at dance.

Today a kind catastrophe allows
The obvious deer to wander simply
For a time. The hunter's bow and arrows
Are laid aside and the complication
His hunger brings: the clearness of the sky
Becomes for him sudden inspirations
Of the wind, a false emptiness to try,

As through forests he unfolds the silence
And careful sanctuary of animals.
The fisherman by ponderous expense
Of net and line would reap from the river,
From its exhausted pools and prodigal
Processions, the fish at rest or spurned
Against the strewing rocks where waters spill.

This morning he forgets to dip and weight
His nets and leaves them to their draping
In the sun. He does not aggravate
The intimate upheavals of fast water
With his splashing boat, nor its quarrelings
With his lonely chant as he pulls the oar.
Today in joy and company he sings.

All days and all their seasons are become
The day and surer seasons of the dance.
And, like a top which spins to make a hum,
Balancing and turning many colours
Into one, the dance's clear emotions
Are mingled through accelerated hours
To phrase the clearer song of its devotions.

Women, filled with the punctual thunder
Hammered on the drums, are huge to handle,
Waiting for love to boil or break or
Come to them quick like a man from a bush.
The hunter's thoughts are ready to descend,
Like perfect arrows for colossal beasts,
To forests of a momentary legend.

The fisherman explores his newest cadence
And, singing, makes a kind of river flow.
After the ruling sun's fierce decadence,
In the slight dominion of the moon
The dance, become its own enclosure, grows
Through enlightened dancers to horizons
Of its dawning and all that sunset knows.

And wearily they turn to celebrate
Tomorrow, through whose rare perfections
The dance's fleeting stations echo late
And always further, as ripples circled
On travelling water which conveys their span,
Run across a progress of brief waves,
In stretching patterns of the wider plan.

MICHAEL LONGLEY

REPORT TO THE DIRECTOR

I'd say their marble cubicles were a shade
Too small for the taller men, but they all appeared
To be standing at ease. O the usual postures—hands
In their pockets, hands on their hips, hands on the wall.
A few touched themselves. A few were saying prayers
Perhaps. I expect a few were feeling the cold
From that bare cement floor in those bedroom slippers.
I did, in my shoes; but still, I suppose one allows
A little latitude in the provinces. No money
To do it all in style. However, it worked
And we did get going. One man was reluctant
To co-operate about buttons—a big fellow
With a lot of weight to throw around: it's always
Annoying that sort of thing: a nasty business
It can be on those tiles. So we gave a hand,
Igor and I. The locals didn't mind,
They rarely do. From there it was plain sailing
To the main business. The five attendants came
All according to the book, well-turned-out men
In their new aprons, with the usual hoses, and a good
Flexible pump. (I gave them marks for that. You know
There's a lot of friction on those grids if they scuffle
When you fit the neck-plates.
It might be worthwhile specifying cable,
Steel-strapped stuff; it would save in the long run.)
Fortunately, we didn't need it: they were all so docile,
Queued and shuffled out with no trouble at all.
Though the line-up was tricky—they'd done the count
    wrong
So we had to use the shoe-horn on a couple.
But after that it was fine: taps on,
Mask fitted, the legs well held, the right grip
And a nice simple injection—I always think
Those gas-cylinders are all wrong. The infusion

Was one of the smoothest I've seen. Evacuation
Very decent. An infinity of freshness
In a little diffusion of bitter carbolic. Rather sweet.
It took about fifteen minutes to get the stories,
And not much mess: they had to scrub the channel
To clear some vomit, otherwise all O.K.
No frills: but at least the operation was completed
With all proper precautions, the doors closed,
The men screened: and, O yes, the windows open
To clean the air. I doubt if anyone smelled
A rat in the whole building, or heard as much
As a squeak from a plimsoll. They moved like
    professionals
From start to finish. I'd say it was all good work.
They certainly do things with the minimum fuss.
I'd recommend we exonerate the whole depot.

                                        GEORGE MACBETH

LOVE POEMS

1

I raise my hands like black wings and feather my hair:
There is nothing I can do to make Catherine Wheels
Or anything, or anyone else beside break you smiles,
A linger like a pearl between me and the sea
Waving, spinikers of sun, a wind
Suddenly up and clean for every coming hour—not
At all for more than shadows in the moon's door.

The daisies in the window-jar bend to listen
To his guitar played in the dark, and someone else's
Head banged up and down for tunes to get you laughing
On and on, and running out of steam, to say,
'Oh that was wonderful,' and say 'yes!' with your look
Long afterward. But what a crazy time it is
To have you flicker up and down, snow on the surf.

Oh, but love is a great thing this way—
To know I cannot kiss you even a little
And have a fire spring in you and stay, high,
Oh high, melt down like a stick of gold, or give you
A hat with daisies on it, or bring you
A glass of water with a cherry in it,
Or pick you up and throw you out the window like a kite.

Where does love go moonward from here? No,
I think it beautiful to play the game,
To be looney in the window with a daisy in my mouth,
And look at you like seas, like grass in a wind,
And high blue breaking out a silken acrobat of gulls—
And then shrug my feathers, arch the failed clown,
And sit down in the window, waiting in your eyes!

2

I have thought of our coming,
The wheeling of gold tendrils together
In a white place, star-circled,
The moon bleeding the pine's amber,
And the blue odor of brooks.

I have thought of our coming in dreams,
And the black light of the sea was there,
My hands passed over the pink shell,
And touched the sand's violet, smoke
That pushed the belly then, and legs
As I crouched down over the embers
Of the shell, in the dark breeze
Where magic is, and the sea moves,
Were moved closer to the sinew
Till it crushed gold, and I fell back,
My arms white branches extended out,
Exquisite pain by the rattling night-grass.

I have thought of our coming
And seen silences in the sea-clouds
Far away over the water,
And refracted in the prism of the lost,
The coiling down sun, me, shaped
Brokenly, still through the shell blown,
The pink-rimmed horn in the grove,
The bent-backward on the pool's rim for sheer
Joy of that pure echo, alight
From the whip of my hair in the dark,
In the sweet touch of the ripples,
News of our coming to the sea beyond this,
News of your coming and mine to the brook,
The odor of amber the wheel of the moon revealed.

MARK MCCLOSKEY

FABLES ABOUT ERROR

I: A RITUAL MOUSE

The mouse in the cupboard repeats himself.
Every morning he lies upside down
Astonished at the violence of the spring
That has tumbled him and the flimsy trap again.
His beady expressionless eyes do not speak
Of the terrible moment we sleep through.
Sometimes a little blood runs from his mouth,
Small and dry like his person.
I throw him into the laurel bush, as being too small
To give the offenses that occasion burial.

It begins to be winter; he is a fieldmouse
And comes in, but how unwisely, from the cold.
Elsewhere now, and from their own points of view,
Cats and poisoners are making the same criticism:
He seems no wiser for having been taken
A dozen nights running. He looks weak;
Given a subtler trap, he might have informed
Or tried to bargain with whatever it is mice have.

Surely there is always that in experience
Which could warn us; and the worst
That can be said of any of us is:
He did not pay attention.

II: A FABLE OF GRACKLES

Like a rift of acrid smoke
A flock of grackles fling in from the river
And fight for the winter sun
Or for seed, is it, in the flailed grass.
Their speech is a mean and endless quarrel

And even in their rising
They keep a sense of strife, flat across the orchard;
Viciousness and greed
Sharpen the spaces of sky between them.

Tonight will bring the dream of fire in the theater
Where rancour drifts through the building
And at the exit, where the screaming should be,
We will trample each other in silence,
And no one get to safety
And no one yield in love.

III: THE TALE OF THE HOUSE SWALLOW ON CAPE ANN

A fluttering bird in the first soft heat of June,
She clung to the feathery elm, swinging and
    swinging,
Inviting a mate from the Massachusetts air.
(Each of us then is but the tally of a creature,
Plato's Aristophanes had said.)

But more than one mate came; they filled the
    warm sky
With dispute of her. For a long, fluttering while
She swayed on the tree-top, alone, swaying.
(The body is always looking for its other,
He said, though it is not bodies alone that mate.)

What she did next made the whole party laugh.
Wanton, we called her, and husbands and wives
    took hands:
She was followed by six males into the dark
    birdhouse.
(In the dark we would solve impulsively the riddle
That even civilized Plato did not get right.)

There was no quarrelling in the birdhouse then.
We went in to dinner. Who hatched those eggs
With her, fed and fledged those little swallows
Aristophanes? Ah, he replies, the ghosting spirit
Is another, more jagged shape. This puzzle is not
    of flesh;

Many people in Massachusetts are moved by lust,
Their hearts yearn for unseemly fittings together
Which their minds disown. Man is aflutter
For the beautiful, Diotima told Socrates,
But the flesh is no more than an instance for the
    mind to consider.

IV: MORAL

What is as wrong as the uninstructed heart?
Left to its ends, it clutches things and creatures
That can't be held, or held, will slip their natures;
It lives to hoard or to protect a hoard.
To school! To school! Teach the poor organ skill
That all its ignorant, nervous will
Does not unpage us like old calendars.
A life should be all gathering and art.

Let there be academies of everything,
That the trap in the warm kitchen yield to guile,
That grackles leave a fire single file,
And swallows find their true halves the first spring.
The mind should be, like art, a gathering
Where the red heart that fumes in the chest
Saying *kill, kill, kill* or *love, love, love.*
Gentled of the need to be possessed,
Can study a little the things that it dreams of.

                          WILLIAM MEREDITH

THE MOSLEMS' ANGEL OF DEATH

(ALGERIA 1961)

Like a jeweled peacock he stirs all over
With fireflies. He takes his pleasure in
Lights.

He is a great honeycomb of shining bees
Knowing every dust with sugar in it.
He has a million fueled eyes.

With all his eyes he explores life.

The firefly city stirs all over with knowledge.
His high buildings see too many
Persons: he has found out
Their times and when their windows
Will go out.

He turns the city lights in his fingers like money.

No other angel knows this one's place,
No other sees his phoenix wings, or understands
That he is lord of Death.

(Death was once allowed
To yell at the sky:
"I am death!
I take friend from friend!
I am death!
l leave your room empty!")

O night, O High Towers! No man can ever
Escape you, O night!

He is a miser. His fingers find the money.
He puts the golden lights in his pocket.

There is one red coal left burning
Beneath the ashes of the great vision.
There is one blood-red eye left open
When the city is burnt out.

Azrael! Azrael!
See the end of trouble!

THOMAS MERTON

PROMOTER

He wakes up in his town, he looks at it,
Hotel Victoria, Bamboo Café, river
Broad as a dream, between willows.
A mad girl
Could float down it any time wreathed in flowers.
He goes to the merchants' luncheons, he is a merchant,
And says, as the long dust stifles roads and meetings
And the springtime day wears on in a tedium of
    dry parity,
Remember, we are on the Avon,
The Canadian Avon;
A poor girl could float down it with flowers,
Rosemary for remembrance.
He doesn't know much about the theater,
But he knows what he likes.

Eventually he goes straight to the watershed,
Of Stratford England, by train and plane,
And brings from his source designers and performers,
So that after the bitter cold lets up,
The plains and streets no longer clogged with snow,
The trilliums again in their coverts,
Tights, doublets, motley come forward from the
    proscenium by the river
And address the members of the Chamber of Commerce.

A Shakespearean teashop thrives on Center Street,
Motels add units.
In rummage and parade, women and children
Move towards fund raising
Othello Braves, Elsinor Indians,
Participating in their own renascence.

Ophelia
Hears the quiet and the drowsy river
A block from town
Murmuring its blank pentameter.
Soft drinks upon the drought of road and field
Bless and are blessed. Yellow buses
Bear in across the plains from larger centers
Hundreds of Torontos in the twilight
In silks, dress kilts, Bermuda shorts.
No place to sleep, they drive through the long midnight,
No place to eat, they picnic in the park,
They are an audience like a sudden, regular
Twice-daily horde; they consume
With a voracity of crickets.

Sometimes as Touchstone is fishing
In the river of the Forest of Arden, the Avon,
A little boy
Alone among the voracious thousands, laughs.
That is his contribution of dollars. The old clowns
Give him back its weight in more fishing.
Such a lot of fishing would upset a show
Were it not Arden.
As it is Arden, a great splash
Splashes in the aisles in the warmth of summer.
Sometimes too the Kings of England flourish,
History recurs; Lancaster reviews his forces,
Richard and Henry in the Chamber of Commerce
Exalt the imagination of their host.

To his ears
Deaf from the winds and roads across Ontario,
Dull with the dusty sounds of dusty voices,
Runs the slow shallow river of the Avon
Carrying yet Ophelia
Speaking her springtime lines into the luncheon

Till he becomes
In some renewed degree, in transformation—
Up to Toronto for funds, over to London,
Back from Moscow with dancers, out of the Bamboo
    Café
For pop in the park—
Orlando,
Comedy's hero in his tent of summer,
Summer's architect in his wide pavilion.

                              JOSEPHINE MILES

SITTING SERIES

1

Who is she?—Just the Marquesa of Carabas
Out sitting on her cold, cold stone;
She's rolled it a long way, and alas
She's rolled it all alone.

O but she's let her hair get all snaggled in the wild
 beachplum
And her feet are streaked with cold!
—Well, she's still a witty wanderer to some
Though, of course, she's getting old.

What's in her hand?—She has a fossil mirror fine
And clear; she asks it, "Tell me true
Will someone miss this face of mine,
Sweet trilobite, as I miss you?"

2

She has been such a long time sitting
Harebells have seeded into her knitting,
Now that the children are all gone
And left her the run of the place alone.

One tall mullein stands like a sceptre!
One lone gull on the bay has kept her
Musing interest: just keeping up there instead
Of *not* is like holding up one's heavy head.

Years have domesticated her Philosopher's Stone;
Quite warm from sun and sitting is this throne
Out in all winds and waters with no need of special
 grace
Once she had rolled it to the heartfelt place.

3

Indoors means a windless working place;
On inevitable table lies *Pencil* who says:
"Mental" to *Inkwell* who says: "Think well!"
To *Pen* who says: ". . . now and then . . ." to
    Paper
Who says: "Rape her."

On wandering *Sill* an *Apple* says: "Windfall"
To *Stairwell* who says: "Harebell" to *Vase*
Who says: "Endless ways . . ." to Canada-blue
Feather who says: "once together . . ."

4

(HER BALLAD)

Pen to paper and push push push
O the poor little bird in the beachplum bush
Was making its song sweet and alone
Till the Boy chipped the shard from the Philosopher's
    Stone.

O the shard glanced off and rolled in the sand
The bird fell into her warm right hand
Feathers and blood were on the knitting
And on the throne where she'd been sitting.

But now how long have I stood alone
Entranced between gull and mullein and stone?
Why does he call me that meaningless name?
Why does he ask me whence I came?

Now the Boy's run off to the cedary part
And the warm little bird I have laid in my heart
But a Cloud has come over—the gull has flown—
And I must push ahead the Philosopher's Stone.

5
(HER PLAIN PROSE PERSONA)

Ah my old prose persona, when he retired from the
 lakes
They brought him his bollard into his bedroom
Along with all sorts of iron things: 2″ spikes,
Marlin spikes, hand-wrought spikes, nails and
 horseshoes
And herring-keg hoops; so what with the nets
 hanging
From the rafters of the loft (they gave him the loft),
And the tarry ropes dangling and the shavings on
 the floor
From his whittling away at things, thinking about
 him
Was like being pulled through all of Robert Louis
 Stevenson
Backward. And in summer when he could look out
 on the 45 degree
Corrugated angles and the weathered shingles of
 the chicken coop
To the orchard with the Astrakhans standing up like
Old Crimea veterans, and when he could rock
 in his rocker,
Mend nets, whistle and spit, and think all sorts of
 sweet thoughts,
One could only hope that all those thoughts were
Shoring up somewhere and doing someone
 somewhere
Some bit of good.

6

—But her feet are rooted in the sand;
It's pitiful, she cannot stand;

Her hair is growing in the thorny tree.
—Her eyes are clear as if they see.

Though stone, she sees the endless ways the
    children run
And jump as if they'll touch the sun,
The way they treadle empty reels as if they'll fly
Before time's done to the endless sky.

M. Morris

INNOCENTS

They paused piously before each cage,
But they did not believe;
For who could believe in the big birch elephant,
The hat-rack elk, or the mangy moulting camels;
Or the giant growling cats, the screaming millinery
    birds?
And most certainly not in the black and rubbery
Slippery seals that jumped six feet from the water.
But little girls held their dolls much tighter,
Kept a respectful distance from the bars,
And some little boys let go of their balloons
To grasp a father's gnarled and tender hand,
Though even he looked doubtful.

PHILIP MURRAY

FOR MY SON, TEN

When it was certain you were lost,
I stumbled up then down the stream,
Shouting your name, and, halting, heard
Your name bound back. As in a dream
You follow yourself with helpless eyes,
I chased my shouts along the bank;
They fluttered back hysterical
Or broken by a cow-bell's clank.
The deer I scattered, birds I sent
Up through dim leaves with frightened news,
The stream I cursed for babbling on,
These had no future world to lose,
Their mindless immortality
Mere evergreen where every glade
Led to your absence. Lost, my call
Went begging, shade by empty shade,
With that name picked when it seemed sure
That, more myself than I, you'd give
My dream a life, but now I swore
To ask nothing but that you live.
And when you found me sitting there
We had our moment after all
In this benighted country, where
One finds his hope beyond recall.
Together, what more is left to ask,
Except my letting go all claim
To what you'll love; the father lost,
Carry, as your own, our name.

LEONARD E. NATHAN

FACE LIFT

You bring me good news from the clinic,
Whipping off your silk scarf, exhibiting the tight white
Mummy-cloths, smiling: I'm all right.
When I was nine, a lime-green anesthetist
Fed me banana gas through a frog-mask. The nauseous vault
Boomed with bad dreams and the Jovian voices of surgeons.
Then mother swam up, holding a tin basin.
O I was sick.

They've changed all that. Traveling
Nude as Cleopatra in my well-boiled hospital shift,
Fizzy with sedatives and unusually humorous,
I roll to an anteroom where a kind man
Fists my fingers for me. He makes me feel something precious
Is leaking from the finger-vents. At the count of two
Darkness wipes me out like chalk on a blackboard . . .
I don't know a thing.

For five days I lie in secret,
Tapped like a cask, the years draining into my pillow.
Even my best friend thinks I'm in the country.
Skin doesn't have roots, it peels away easy as paper.
When I grin, the stitches tauten. I grow backward. I'm twenty,
Broody and in long skirts on my first husband's sofa, my fingers
Buried in the lambswool of the dead poodle;
I hadn't a cat yet.

Now she's done for, the dewlapped lady
I watched settle, line by line, in my mirror—
Old sock-face, sagged on a darning egg.
They've trapped her in some laboratory jar.
Let her die there, or wither incessantly for the next fifty years,
Nodding and rocking and fingering her thin hair.
Mother to myself, I wake swaddled in gauze,
Pink and smooth as a baby.

Sylvia Plath

PRIVATE GROUND

First frost, and I walk among the rose-fruit, the
    marble toes
Of the Greek beauties you brought
Off Europe's relic heap
To sweeten your neck of the New York woods.
Soon each white lady will be boarded up
Against the cracking climate.

All morning, with smoking breath, the handyman
Has been draining the goldfish ponds.
They collapse like lungs, the escaped water
Threading back, filament by filament, to the pure
Platonic table where it lives. The baby carp
Litter the mud like orangepeel.

Eleven weeks, and I know your estate so well
I need hardly go out at all.
A superhighway seals me off.
Trading their poisons, the north and south bound cars
Flatten the doped snakes to ribbon. In here, the grasses
Unload their griefs on my shoes,

The woods creak and ache, and the day forgets itself.
I bend over this drained basin where the small fish
Flex as the mud freezes.
They glitter like eyes, and I collect them all.
Morgue of old logs and old images, the lake
Opens and shuts, accepting them among its reflections.

                                    Sylvia Plath

WUTHERING HEIGHTS

The horizons ring me like faggots,
Tilted and disparate, and always unstable.
Touched by a match, they might warm me,
And their fine lines singe
The air to orange
Before the distances they pin evaporate,
Weighting the pale sky with a solider color.
But they only dissolve and dissolve
Like a series of promises, as I step forward.

There is no life higher than the grasstops
Or the hearts of sheep, and the wind
Pours by like destiny, bending
Everything in one direction.
I can feel it trying
To funnel my heat away.
If I pay the roots of the heather
Too close attention, they will invite me
To whiten my bones among them.

The sheep know where they are,
Browsing in their dirty wool-clouds,
Grey as the weather.
The black slots of their pupils take me in.
It is like being mailed into space,
A thin, silly message.
They stand about in grandmotherly disguise,
All wig curls and yellow teeth
And hard, marbly baas.

I come to wheel ruts, and water
Limpid as the solitudes
That flee through my fingers.
Hollow doorsteps go from grass to grass;

Lintel and sill have unhinged themselves.
Of people the air only
Remembers a few odd syllables.
It rehearses them moaningly:
Black stone, black stone.

The sky leans on me, me, the one upright
Among all horizontals.
The grass is beating its head distractedly.
It is too delicate
For a life in such company;
Darkness terrifies it.
Now, in valleys narrow
And black as purses, the house lights
Gleam like small change.

SYLVIA PLATH

DIVISION

During the winter she began
   to notice things coming apart,
   dividing with no special plan
   into slabs and rounds. At the heart
   of the wind that blew in the street,
   below the lengths of tan coffee
   smell, and river, and oily, sweet
   burning chicken bubbled the tree-
   sour flavor of wine. In the round,
   barking throats of dogs, stone teeth ground.

When she went inside, the heads,
   the arms, the eyes rained down on her
   in a shower of sound; the reds,
   the deep bone grays were a blur
   of noise—so loud that the ends
   of her fingers became smooth and numb.
   She could only speak to her friends,
   she found, in a long, narrow hum
   of transparent sound.

                    One evening,
   moving quickly, simply trying
   to make things whole, she got naked
   onto an uptown bus, and would
   not be hidden, would not be led;
   and when they dragged her off, she could
   see the lean tree of their arms spread
   out and could hear each color they said.

                           JOHN RATTI

THE FAR FIELD

I

I dream of journeys repeatedly:
Of flying like a bat deep into a narrowing tunnel,
Of driving alone, without luggage, out a long peninsula,
The road lined with snow-laden second growth,
A fine dry snow ticking the windshield,
Alternate snow and sleet, no on-coming traffic,
And no lights behind, in the blurred side-mirror,
The road changing from glazed tarface to a rubble of
    stone,
Ending at last in a hopeless sand-rut,
Where the car stalls,
Churning in a snowdrift
Until the headlights darken.

II

At the field's end, in the corner missed by the mower,
Where the turf drops off into a grass-hidden culvert,
Haunt of the cat-bird, nesting-place of the field-mouse,
Not too far away from the ever-changing flower-dump,
Among the tin cans, tires, rusted pipes, broken
    machinery,—
One learned of the eternal;
And in the shrunken face of a dead rat, eaten by rain
    and ground-beetles
(I found it lying among the rubble of an old coal bin)
And the tom-cat, caught near the pheasant-run,
Its entrails strewn over the half-grown flowers,
Blasted to death by the night watchman.

I suffered for birds, for young rabbits caught in the
    mower,
My grief was not excessive.
For to come upon warblers in early May
Was to forget time and death:
How they filled the oriole's elm, a twittering restless
    cloud, all one morning,
And I watched and watched till my eyes blurred from the
    bird shapes,—
Cape May, Blackburnian, Cerulean,—
Moving, elusive as fish, fearless,
Hanging, bunched like young fruit, bending the end
    branches,
Still for a moment,
Then pitching away in half-flight,
Lighter than finches,
While the wrens bickered and sang in the half-green
    hedgerows,
And the flicker drummed from his dead tree in the
    chicken-yard.

—Or to lie naked in sand,
In the silted shallows of a slow river,
Fingering a shell,
Thinking:
Once I was something like this, mindless,

Or perhaps with another mind, less peculiar;
Or to sink down to the hips in a mossy quagmire;
Or, with skinny knees, to sit astride a wet log,
Believing:
I'll return again,
As a snake or a raucous bird,
Or, with luck, as a lion.

I learned not to fear infinity,
The far field, the windy cliffs of forever,
The dying of time in the white light of tomorrow,
The wheel turning away from itself,
The sprawl of the wave,
The on-coming water.

III

The river turns on itself,
The tree retreats into its own shadow.
I feel a weightless change, a moving forward
As of water quickening before a narrowing channel
When banks converge, and the wide river whitens;
Or when two rivers combine, the blue glacial torrent
And the yellowish-green from the mountainy upland,—
At first a swift rippling between rocks,
Then a long running over flat stones

Before descending to the alluvial plain,
To the clay banks, and the wild grapes hanging from the
 elmtrees,
The slightly trembling water
Dropping a fine yellow silt where the sun stays;
And the crabs bask near the edge,
The weedy edge, alive with small snakes and
 bloodsuckers,—

I have come to a still, but not a deep center,
A point outside the glittering current;
My eyes stare at the bottom of a river,
At the irregular stones, iridescent sandgrains,
My mind moves in more than one place,
In a country half-land, half-water.

I am renewed by death, thought of my death,
The dry scent of a dying garden in September,
The wind fanning the ash of a low fire.
What I love is near at hand,
Always, in earth and air.

IV

The lost self changes,
Turning toward the sea,
A sea-shape turning around,—
An old man with his feet before the fire,
In robes of green, in garments of adieu.

A man faced with his own immensity
Wakes all the waves, all their loose wandering fire.
The murmur of the absolute, the why
Of being born fails on his naked ears.
His spirit moves like monumental wind
That gentles on a sunny blue plateau.
He is the end of things, the final man.

All finite things reveal infinitude:
The mountain with its singular bright shade
Like the blue skies on freshly frozen snow,
The after-light upon ice-burdened pines;
Odor of basswood on a mountain-slope,
A scent beloved of bees;
Silence of water above a sunken tree:
The pure serene of memory in one man,—
A ripple widening from a single stone
Winding around the waters of the world.

THEODORE ROETHKE

THE HARE

The long view first, the distant scene:
A moving splotch of brown on green;
A hare-because-he-must-be-hare,
For what else brown could be feeding there?

Then middle-distance hare-by-shape;
Hare by his long-eared long-legged lope;
Hare by the way he stands up straight
With forepaws bent as though he were praying,
But the tilt of his head as he looks about
And the flare of his eyes at once denying
His pantomime humility;
And hare in his crouch as a hawk flies over,
Belly so low in the short white clover
That a pattern of leaves only three inches high
Breaks the line of his back to the hawk in the sky;
And hare while he crawls with ears tucked down
To a clump of dead grass that matches his brown
Where he hides from the hawk who is out to seek
No more than a cricket to fill his beak:

And last the close-up in a squat:
Each-hair-detailed hare-by-Dürer;
And difficult now when he should be clearer
For brown unbrowns to grey and white,
Black and cream and brown, and light
So confuses tone and shadow,
And the long hairs spiked from his tidy coat
Like his whiskers tremble so,
It makes him somewhat indistinct;
And when side-on I meet his eye,
As black and full as a muscat grape,
Fixed in a deep unblinking stare,
It bares such urgent life within
That the eye rates more and the body less
Till like some ancient birth from chaos
There is one live eye in a waste of hare.

Eric C. Rolls

NELSON AT PALERMO

Monte Pellegrino, mauve, bald and granite skull
That holds Palermo in vast dull
Shade, entrapped the langours and the heat
Of summer in the golden shell whose neat
Cubed villas lay where waters lapped
The Porta Felice and its trapped
And groaning court; the Bourbon King and Queen,
Sir William H., rickety Pantaloon,
And Nelson, Harlequin to Columbine.
The *coup de foudre* can strike at any time,
It seems; one-armed, one-eyed and 39
Years aged with fevers, ague and wounds
He felt himself a fox pursued by hounds,
Courtiers, lazzarini, C-in-C's. Before the kill,
Though, in his arm the beloved vixen lay.

A sailor lives by names: the Nile, Aboukir Bay,
Boreas, Vanguard, Foudroyant, and here,
Inactive at a foreign court, the one
Most potent of them all, 'dear Lady Hamilton',
Become, by stages now impenetrable, 'my love',
'My darling angel'. 'Ever for ever, I am yours,
Only yours, Even beyond this world'. The one
Word *Emma* joins the names of ships,
The buoyant prow attached to dazzling lips.

Fireworks at La Favorita, *fêtes champêtres*,
Hard gales, and after supper at La Nova,
Faro into the dawn. The non-playing hero fell asleep,
The look of love a film across the eyes.
The day began at five. No wonder Orpheus nods.
Cards are for ambassadresses, not for gods.

Palm trees, oranges, ochre and grey pavilions.
Ennui sustained by passion. Emma bloomed.
Together, in small tavernas, side by side
They watched the drunken sailors reel on board,
'Viva Nelson' the cry when they were recognized.
At Palazzo Palagonia champagne flowed,
Night after night: revolution here was stayed,

With public hangings watched by thronging crowds.
Nelson might fidget, hate the climate
And that illiberal bore, the Queen, but *she*
Was antidote to civil servants, frets, the rain:
The noose of thraldom stronger than the pain
Of having to choose, of making his interest plain.

ALAN ROSS

THE FORTRESS

(WHILE TAKING A NAP WITH LINDA)

Under the pink quilted covers,
I hold the pulse that counts your blood.
I think the woods outdoors
are half asleep,
left over from summer
like a stack of books after a flood,
left over like the promises I never keep.
On the right, the scrub pine tree
waits like a fruit store
holding up bunches of tufted broccoli.

We watch the wind from our square bed.
I press down my index finger,
half in jest, half in dread,
on the brown mole
under your left eye, inherited
from my right cheek—a spot of danger
where a bewitched worm ate its way through our soul
in search of beauty. Child, since July
the leaves have been fed
secretly from a pool of beet-red dye.

And sometimes they are battle green
with trunks as wet as hunters' boots,
smacked hard by the wind, clean
as oilskins. No,
the wind's not off the ocean.
Yes, it cried in your room like a wolf
and your ponytail hurt you. That was a long time ago.
The wind rolled the tide like a dying
woman. She wouldn't sleep;
she rolled there all night, grunting and sighing.

Darling, life is not in my hands;
life with its terrible changes
will take you, bombs or glands,
your own child at
your breast, your own house on your own land.
Outside, the bittersweet turns orange.
Before she died, my mother and I picked those fat
branches, finding orange nipples
on the gray wire strands.
We weeded the forest, curing trees like cripples.

Your feet thump-thump against my back
and you whisper to yourself. Child,
what are you wishing? What pact
are you making?
What mouse runs between your eyes? What ark
can I fill for you when the world goes wild?
The woods are under water, their weeds are shaking
in the tide; birches like zebra fish
flash by in a pack.
Child, I cannot promise that you will get your wish.

I cannot promise very much.
I give you the images I know.
Lie still with me and watch.
A pheasant moves
by like a seal, pulled through the mulch
by his thick white collar. He's on show
like a clown. He drags a beige feather that he
    removed,
one time, from an old lady's hat.
We laugh and we touch.
I promise you love. Time will not take away that.

                              ANNE SEXTON

LAKE CHELAN

They call it regional, this relevance—
the deepest place we have: in this pool forms
the model of our land, a lonely one,
responsive to the wind. Everything we own
has brought us here: from here we speak.

The sun stalks among these peaks to sight
the lake down aisles, long like a gun;
a ferryboat, lost by a century, toots
for trappers, the pelt of the mountains
rinsed in the sun and that sound.

Suppose a person far off to whom this lake
occurs: told a problem, he might hear a word
so dark he drowns an instant, and stands dumb
for the centuries of his country and the suave
hills beyond the stranger's sight.

Is this man dumb, then, for whom Chelan lives
in the wilderness? On the street you've seen
someone like a trapper's child pause,
and fill his eyes with some irrelevant flood—
a tide stops him, delayed in his job.

Permissive as a beach, he turns inland,
harks like a fire, glances through the dark
like an animal drinking, and arrives along that line
a lake has found far back in the hills,
the brim gravity exactly requires.

WILLIAM STAFFORD

RHINOCEROS

I have never seen that beast,
with his snout bearing a pagoda
and his eyes like little fragments
and his haunches carrying hills
with them. His teeth, I have read,
are monuments, and his heart colder
than a key in winter,
though he sweats from pores round
    as goblets
and full of swamps.
The white hunters have killed him
a thousand times over.

I think of myself walking toward him
and preaching a love of creatures,
leaves in my palm, or a loaf of sugar,
and his great horn still,
the knees waiting,
and between us, like birds,
a twittering hope,
or merely the pause
between monster and monster.

                    Adrien Stoutenburg

WEIGHING THE HEART OF THE SCRIBE ANI

Ani, an Egyptian, understood the insecurity of death.
How staying home was going home,
How urn and oil and beer were necessary
In the underworld of wonders.

The walls of Ani's expensive tomb display
Life's everydayness: the business of the larder and
    the laundry,
The panic of sudden hunger should all this fail him.
And elongated servants, pale as charity,
Stand stiff surrounded by so much horde and plenty.

Ani, the Scribe, washed his heart
In the murmur of the Nile as he lay
Sickening for death. When it was over
And while the embalmers were shriveling
His skin to last forever, Ani and his wife
Entered together into the judgment hall,
A shrine of fire and living serpents that rests
Upon a stream of water.
Osiris, maker of gods, the king of south and north,
Sat behind the scale of judgment watching.
The platters of his scale carried on one side
A feather, and on the other Ani's heart
Bearing its virtues like medals in aluminum, or lighter.

How diminutive a man is that a feather
Could outweigh his essence and his juices,
His righteousness and fury,
And his marriage to a priestess.

Ani's wife stood wringing her paper hands
Unable to prophesy or pray his ordeal over.
Am-mit, Eater of the dead, crouched
Ready to devour the heart in a single pounce
Should Osiris find it lighter, lacking, or uncomely.

But Ani's heart was heavy, and he lay staring
    through his mummy
For years before the robbers came.
Bearing him no malice, they stole
His urns and oil, the necklaces and rings
From the coil of his neck and from his fingers, dry
    as old cigars.
Then they hacked him up into the pieces
Of a puzzle and threw him, bandages and all,
To their hungry camels who had sat folded up
All night in the hollows of the dunes.

                      NANCY SULLIVAN

SEVEN OCCASIONS FOR SONG

I wish to make a speech on singing birds.
Unfortunately I make my speech in words,
Balanced on a cushion instead of a wing.
But, having been birds' friend and enemy,
Owning a tree and an anthology,
I know why birds sing.

Some sing to sing. Whether endowed
With fine or pitiable voices, they crowd
Heaven extempore, singing their sense
That sense involves a gut's mystique, and sound
Means melody. They exercise around
Each other, assuring themselves an audience.

Some sing to find out who they are,
And having found, they make a lyric game
Of calling themselves their own, their favorite name,
Until, alone, they feel like a seminar.
Their interest in themselves is genuine
Again, and again, and again, and again, and again.

Some trill brilliantly for sex
Employing a hundred kindred arts and tricks
Of dancing, rhetoric, and politics;
Fearful of remaining virginal wrecks
They sometimes sing their hearts out protesting
Love, loathing music, and hearts, and nesting.

Some, the delicately young and delicately old,
Call requesting comfort for their cold
Bodies and provisional minds among the seething
Currents of inhabited air, before flight
And after. They seek a small song breathing
Like sleep, before dawn, after night.

Some shout aggression, staking the land
They are, by God, determined to command;
They strike their boundaries of wormed sod
And infected space, refusing to defer
To any other feathers, including God:
Song is a dare wreaked out of anger.

Some trembling wary sentinels,
Skilled at reading a shadow's portents
Sing warning the race of enduring troubles
Inhabiting home's furtive elements;
They cry, "Beware," for horrors which hover, glide,
Tramp the world. They cry, "Beware," and hide.

And some sing a gathering call
After danger. As if danger had quit
The world for birds and song could forestall
Death, they sing a ceremony of infinite
Sky and a quiet tree and a day long
As life, shining, utterly fit for song.

And seven occasions become one occasion
And every bird sings from seven throats
His seven heavenly sins of every season;
Knowing he sings with only human vision
Composed of human measures and human notes
He finally sings for no final reason.

HOLLIS SUMMERS

PIGEON WOMAN

Slate, or dirty-marble-colored,
or rusty-iron-colored, the pigeons
on the flagstones in front of the
Public Library make a sharp lake

into which the pigeon woman wades
at exactly 1:30. She wears a
plastic pink raincoat with a round
collar (looking like a little

girl, so gay) and flat gym shoes,
her hair square-cut orange.
Wide-apart feet carefully enter
the spinning, crooning waves

(as if she'd just learned how
to walk, each step conscious,
an accomplishment) blue knots in the
calves of her bare legs (uglied marble),

age in angled cords of jaw
and neck, her pimento-colored hair,
hanging in thin tassels, is gray
around a balding crown.

The day-old bread drops down
from her veined hand dipping out
of a paper sack. Choppy, shadowy ripples,
the pigeons strike around her legs.

Sack empty, she squats and seems to rinse
her hands in them—the rainy greens and
oily purples of their necks. Almost
they let her wet her thirsty fingertips—

but drain away in an untouchable tide.
A make-believe trade
she has come to, in her lostness
or illness or age—to treat the motley

city pigeons at 1:30 every day, in all
weathers. It is for them she colors
her own feathers. Ruddy-footed
on the lime-stained paving,

purling to meet her when she comes,
they are a lake of love. Retreating
from her hands as soon as empty,
they are the flints of love.

May Swenson

THE ALBINO MAN

The albino man came through my gate at dawn, and I
Breath-caught, stood at my window wondering.
He held a sun-mote on his finger like a bird,
Perched on the rim of his finger like a bird,
Bright-polled, singing.
At his heels came a black hound with a silver tail
And a collar of silver, and silver claws,
Silently, silently, as if it walked air-borne.
Where the man walked in that dew of grass
No blade bent and no leaf moved,
But his muscles moved, under his skin, like wine,
And his eyes, strong with cold, saw the juice of the
    leaf,
Saw the thick sweet sap in the tree heart,
The quartz molecule in the tiny pebble,
Saw the sun's eye in lambent dew twig-held,
The old bullet rusting six feet down,
Saw the loneliness at my doorsill,
The old despair in my empty hall,
Saw me!
Was it yesterday or years ago he came?
I do not know; I could not let him in.

                          Lilian Symons

THE WELL

There is an indelible well somewhere, deep in blue-
    veined quartz, opaquely crystal
Under quiescent trees, softly shaded, and smelling of
    lavender.
Or beneath the dolphin waves, octopus-guarded,
With a ring of golden sea horses and a deep blue light.

There is a well at the desultory crossroads
Where wild carrot takes the field in riot and moon-
    faced daisies
Bucolic in their tastes, eddy in the tide of happenstance,
And one tree, broken-armed,
Waves a red banner of hips and haws,
Or in the monotonous wheat rolling in deep monotone
A cryptic dactylology of wheretofind.

There is a matutinal well somewhere, deep as the iron
    earth's core,
Liplevel full of whys and itching wheres and whens,
But calm as an empty mirror, ice-leaf cool and deep
With the ultimate answers.

I have searched for it with witches and warlocks,
With simpletons and sirs and smooth-tongued sages
And a tame tiger, broken-footed, with sad green eyes.
I have sought it in despair in my love's rich green grove
And wept.
In the sea-deeps and the bronze-green shallows,
I have overturned great shells of mother-of-pearl,
    questing,

And duelled with swordfish deep in a chartless cave
Where eerie witchlight glowed on walls of chalk.
In freckled country lanes, milky with late afternoon,
In silken cities, bored with old wine, in jungles
And iron-capped cellars echoing with pain,
I have questioned time, with desperate patience
And a tame tiger, broken-footed, with sad green eyes.
There is a well somewhere in a pilot valley,
Brave with old knowledge and deep with pitiful ferns.

Or is it in the mountains,
Deep-walled with ancient snows that tremble with
    unaccustomed sun,
Rumbling with terrible anguish, suddenly awakening?
I shall go to meet the juggernaut avalanche,
I shall drink from the peaceful well in the avalanche
With my tame tiger, broken-footed and wise green-eyed.

LILIAN SYMONS

HEAVEN

In the heaven of the god I hope for (call him X)
There is marriage and giving in marriage and
    transient sex
For those who will cast the body's vest aside
Soon, but are not yet wholly rarefied
And still embrace. For X is never annoyed
Or shocked; has read his Jung and knows his Freud.
He gives you time in heaven to do as you please,
To climb love's gradual ladder by slow degrees,
Gently to rise from sense to soul, to ascend
To a world of timeless joys, world without end.

Here on the gates of pearl there hangs no sign
Limiting cakes and ale, forbidding wine.
No weakness here is hidden, no vice unknown.
Sin is a sickness to be cured, outgrown
With the help of a god who can laugh, an unsolemn
    god
Who smiles at old wives' tales of iron rod
And fiery hell, a god who's more at ease
With bawds and Falstaffs than with pharisees.

Here the lame learn to leap, the blind to see.
Tyrants are taught to be humble, slaves to be free.
Fools become wise and wise men cease to be bores.
Here bishops learn from lips of back-street whores,
And white men follow black-faced angels' feet
Through fields of orient and immortal wheat.

Villon, Lautrec and Baudelaire are here.
Here Swift forgets his anger, Poe his fear.
Napoleon rests. Columbus, journeys done,
Has reached his new Atlantis, found his sun.
Verlaine and Dylan Thomas drink together.
Marx talks to Plato. Byron wonders whether

There's some mistake. Wordsworth has found a hill
That's home. Here Chopin plays the piano still.
Wren plans ethereal domes; and Renoir paints
Young girls as ripe as fruit but not yet saints.

And X, of whom no coward is afraid,
Who's friend consulted, not fierce king obeyed;
Who hears the unspoken thought, the prayer
    unprayed;
Who expects not even the learned to understand
His universe, extends a prodigal hand,
Full of forgiveness, over his promised land.

A. S. J. Tessimond

A LIGHT OF REVELATION
TO THE GENTILES

Not as when she darted in and out
among the willows like the waters
of Shiloh running softly does she
go up to Bethlehem. Nor lithely
as a March wind ago when she swung
the water jar up to her hairs' dark
iridescence and sped home to that

shaft of pure spirit in her door. His
words were bells that rang the centuries
pendant to this timeless moment when
under the shadow of Jehovah
she who was scarcely ripe to girlhood
found herself wonderful with child.
Then from Aries to Capricorn

in the pull of her tides she braided
the dayspring feeding him silence, till
billowed like a small white sail blowing
to port, she beaches in the chalk cave's
sharpest shadow. And what woman who
has born (or not born) but knows her flesh
leap with light to see Mary reach from

her cloak the little woven things, and
while hushed seas and islands wait—from
out the bright tegument of her body
unswaddle the *shekinah*, and to
the young Joseph (helpless as any
man at such a moment) turn her face
smiling and hold up the Morning Star.

Sister M. Therese

THE DAY BEFORE THE LAST

The soil was tougher, stonier to the spade
In the new-broken field, and so he laboured
Long into evening. The air turned cold;
His hands ached, and he'd missed a favourite
    programme.
No angel came
To tell him this was unneeded, pointless work
—For all his holy trade—that he might have rested.
And now the expensive earth stood piled high.

Over this earth, and over the spilled churchyard
The sun was setting, as it always had—
Shedding a peaceful, ordinary light
On the closed community of simple graves.
Nothing to tell. Nothing to tell the world
This was the end, the very last of its sunsets;
And the new field in vain.

If there was a sign, if we had only known
On that brown-eyed day in September
(Not yet the end of British Summer Time)
That time itself was a departing guest,
We'd have cried in the streets, and faltered tears of
    passion,
To see the crimson go out of the last sky . . .
If we had known, we'd surely have done *something*.

Instead, we drank our coffee and went upstairs,
And said a prayer by rote perhaps—and slept.
The day had been—you understand?—so normal,
And so tomorrow would be. Nothing said:
'No more the spade to earth, the hand to plough;
This is the twilight Eden, more endeared
By human love, and its most precious dust.'

                                          D. M. Thomas

LINES FOR MY GRANDMOTHER'S GRAVE

When she died at last it was in the fall of the year
Outside her window the children going to school
Passed with long shadows morning and afternoon

Boys in the street ran at football and piled their sweaters
Carelessly on the curb the little girls
Minded the solemn baby in his carriage

In the lingering twilight of the apartment houses
Out of those sour backyards no harvest was gathered
But the bins in the supermarket were full of fruit

Far off on the avenue behind the windows
Of the expensive shops all the lifelike figures
Scented and hatted and furred achieved nirvana

Enclosed in eternal ennui they are immortal

Darkness fell early but night was slow in coming
Where they bolstered her in a chair no saccharine vision
Of lavender-fragrant old age in a cloudy halo

In the tight little bedroom of the nursing-home
Where the scrubbing-brush fought against the smell of
    mortality
She ruled like the empress of an angry island

Pitching her voice against those who refused to hear her
The joints of her fingers swelled with indignation
She tossed on the ocean of her recollections

Long ago in the rocking boat she came with the eldest
Over the edge of the world because she had to
And had to forget the world behind her back

Because only tomorrow she knew is truly immortal

Her children's children were never real to her
When they brought her presents although she tried to
    thank them
And her husband these forty years or more in the grave

Had turned to a fiction although he had left her
A houseful of chattering strangers to worry over
Grieving to think of the endless parade of tomorrows

Marching along toward unspecified destinations
In the gathering dusk anticipating night
Perpetually at bay outside the windows

After she died they found she had written poems
In the language of her girlhood that they could not read
And were partly ashamed of to think that she had not
    forgotten

But they marked her grave with a stone which is
    immortal

Constance Urdang

TRIADS

Who am I to load the year with continual
    misunderstanding?
I will not accuse winter of a protracted hardness,
Nor spring of callousness, nor summer of regret.

The oak-leaf changes: green gloss cups the acorn.
First hidden, then emerging from resistance to statement,
The fruit holds nothing in its fullness but the tree.

To have held through hail, stormwinds, and black frost
    in darkness
Through the long months, gives meaning to the bud
    when it opens.
Song loses nothing of moments that are past.

So my labour is still: it is still determination
To resolve itself slowly in the weathers of knowledge.
By virtue of the hidden the poem is revealed.

Remember Earth's triads: the faith of a dumb animal,
The mountain stream falling, music to the wheat-ears;
The salt wave echoing the grieving of the bones.

The lamb leaps: it is stubborn in its innocence.
The hawk drops, in the energy of instinct.
Dawn fires kindle perfection like a sword.

Fires: the hawk's talons, the tongue of the chameleon,
In a peacock's wings' lightning the contraction of glory,
In death the last miracle, the unconditional gift.

What do I need but patience before the unpredictable,
The endurance of the stepping-stone before the
    footprint,
Cadence that reconciles wisdom and the dance?

I need more, I need more. In the moment of perception
Fit me, prayer, to lose everything, that nothing may
    be lost.
The stone that accumulates history is falling.

History is a pageant, and all men belong to it.
We die into each other: remember how many
Confided their love, not in vain, to the same earth.

VERNON WATKINS

HARRY

It's the day for writing that letter, if one is able,
And so the striped institutional shirt is wedged
Between this holy holy chair and table.
He has purloined paper, he has begged and cadged
The bent institutional pen,
The ink. And our droll old men
Are darting constantly where he weaves his sacrament.

Sacrifice? Propitiation? All are blent
In the moron's painstaking fingers—so painstaking,
His vestments our giddy yarns of the firmament,
Women, gods, electric trains, and our remaking
Of all known worlds—but not yet
Has our giddy alphabet
Perplexed his priestcraft and spilled the cruet of
     innocence.

We have been plucked from the world of commonsense,
Fondling between our hands some shining loot,
Wife, mother, beach, fisticuffs, eloquence,
As the lank tree cherishes every distorted shoot.
What queer shards we could steal
Shaped him, realer than the Real:
But it is no goddess of ours guiding the fingers and the
     thumb.

She cries: *Ab aeterno ordinata sum.*
He writes to the woman, this lad who will never marry.
One vowel and the thousand laborious serifs will come
To this pudgy Christ, and the old shape of Mary.
Before seasonal pelts and the thin
Soft tactile underskin
Of air were stretched across earth, they have sported
     and are one.

Was it then at this altar-stone the mind was begun?
The image besieges our Troy. Consider the sick
Convulsions of movement, and the featureless baldy sun
Insensible—sparing that compulsive nervous tic.
Before life, the fantastic succession,
An imbecile makes his confession,
Is filled with the Word unwritten, has almost
    genuflected.

Because the wise world has for ever and ever rejected
Him and because your children would scream at the
    sight
Of his mongol mouth stained with food, he has
    resurrected
The spontaneous though retarded and infantile light.
Transfigured with him we stand
Among walls of the no-man's-land
While he licks the soiled envelope with a lover's caress

Directing it to the House of no known address.

FRANCIS WEBB

SALAMANDER

Not a fixed ceremonial date but some
Familiar and moving sign
Should mark the beginning of a season.

The spring here could be marked beginning
Any day after Christmas with the flowering quince
Or as late as late April with the cherry.

I choose for a spring signal on my hill
The first land-wandering water-dog, usually
In early March they are coming up the orchard,
Prowling along the roadway and the porches.

Orange to umber, they are all colours of rust,
Fall colours, but they move with determination,
As green-driven as any sprout or bud.

The first water-dog this year was an old one,
Skin the colour of redwood bark and as rough.

Although they travel on fiery affairs
The little ones look lost away from water.

But this big one, derelict-iron dry and dark,
Reminds me: the ancestral salamander, whether
By gills, lungs, or a lost alchemy, was a fire-breather.

And not of the fountain-fires, the green
Bud fires, leaf fires, rain-kindled fires of spring

But of that original fire, element
Before rumours of water or the fact of earth.

Reminds me: the world has been a sphere of flame,
Spinning without darkness in the universe,
Shadowless, timeless, winterless, lifeless.

This spring that we believe an ancient season,
Calling it new only as it returns;
Our little vision and vast calculation,
My world, your world, this world
Came suddenly with cooling, casting shadow,—

Suddenly, recently, possibly only briefly.

Not a fixed ceremonial date, but some
Familiar and moving symbol
Should mark the beginning of a season

So, on my hill, the first land-wandering water-dog,
The recent fire-breather, salamander,
For yet another spring for this green planet,
For this young shade in the old glare of star sight.

MARIE DE L. WELCH

THE SPACE FLIER

And now he is dressed, snugly and with care,
Buttoned, muffled and padded as by
His mother's hands, to face the snow outdoors.

He strides into a dazzling light like snow,
Arc-lights that blot his shadow, the rustle of faces
Peering, applauding, make a gauntlet of his path

Shimmering to the steel rungs. The man is calm as
    he climbs.
The crowd quietens, admiring their uncertainty,
And no one rubs his charmed eyes to reflect

How gradually a man, groping, achieves himself,
Painfully, as the touch of his life infects,
Poisons at his fingertips the burst stone and the burnt

Cherry-tree, the millions dead, greater than numbers
    of stars;
And the risk that stutters in the winking eyes
Of his steel crib, past breath of straw and

Cattle in Christ's manger. And now,
If nothing blunders, his life will flower
Too suddenly, like a tulip with false heat,

A botanist's trick, to catch the applause
Of wits and innocents, to throw ambition
Reliefed against the sky where he is the hunter

Jacklighting with the slow hook of his flight
The risky shapes that break
His night's surface like corks, subside with a splash

And vanish. But his dangers, they say
Are charted, planned with care; it is their hearts,
The watchers, that leap

Far higher than he can go, down into the profound
Uncertainty of their skulls swollen to take
No new knowledge, but to confirm old fears,

The reticence of a lame man, of a snowballing boy
Whose fingers freeze against the injuring chance
To act. And none pity him—

It is themselves they pity. The fires
That could lick him up are tongues they'd praise
    him with,
Like scolding mothers, scorning their failure, a man

Whose nature, betraying their effort, would steal
Quick grief by his downfall, and be memorialized,
His cinder to stone. But now none pity him—

'See, this is a tough one!' the watchers shout,
'His arching snowball will not melt in his hands',
And watch the fire of his trajectory scorching higher

Beyond tangent and compass of their suffering.

DAVID WEVILL

AFTER THE SNAKE

After the snake had been mastered, cobra of words
hoodface swaying to flute, or a python thought
shot on the branch before involvement could crush,
or the sidewinder mind detected and cunningly
    caught—
alive by my door, looped in a diamond hush,
I saw the serpent I had read about.

It had crept to a vine-cool corner where water
    dripped,
from the day's heat, a dreaded length at rest,
gifted with guile, mottled, watching from slits
in lidless eyes, illicit as Eden's pest,
and yet, in variety's garden, who has the right
to judge the wanted or unwanted guest?

Prodded, it slenderly slid, as much fearing
as feared, and tasting intention with a nervous
    thread,
slowly unwinding, tried to disappear.
A symbol would have smiled, a rattler coiled;
this visitor only desired the nearness of water
and didn't guess his simple presence chilled.

But such suggestions hardly ever can slip
back to secure obscurity once they come out.
Terror will have a hand with an ax to grip—
such is appearance's strength and power of doubt
that not until after the snake we mistake has been
    killed
does dazed regret gaze in the fangless mouth.

                      HAROLD WITT

METAMORPHOSIS

Cicadas sizzling on the spit
of summer feel the season turn
them round and round in juicy fat,
in succulence of dripping song.
How neat and fleet the fiddles burn
their melting flesh, a gone-to-hell-
and-mad-and-merry carrousel
tells August she's a fading blonde.

Tells August what the fiddles know
of lines in undertaker black:
the buzzard, beetle, carrion crow
will strip her grain by grain until
these feasting kleptomaniacs
sink claws and jaws, and withered crone
is shin and shank and collar bone
they strew like toothpicks through the hills.

There goes a shawl of wind blown birds
with fledgling song, and as wine pours
through August's fingers, the absurd
fat bellies pop from purple grapes;
Through spitting seed the music soars
triumphant heights; then on the trees,
still hanging by their fiddling knees,
I count these crisp mute shells of shape.

Exta Williams Wolking